to Eva,

love, Opa :

STORIES
WE
SHARED

A FAMILY BOOK JOURNAL

for the storytellers

STORIES WE SHARED: A FAMILY BOOK JOURNAL © 2016 Douglas Kaine McKelvey & Jamin Still

Published by
RABBIT ROOM PRESS
3321 Stephens Hill Lane
Nashville, Tennessee 37013
info@rabbitroom.com

Illustrations © 2016 by Jamin Still   Text © 2016 by Douglas Kaine McKelvey

ISBN 978-0-9983112-0-3

The cover illustration is a detail of the painting *The Sea of Fields*, from the Rabbit Room Press picture book *The Wishes of the Fish King*, illustrated by Jamin Still, text by Douglas Kaine McKelvey.

RABBIT ROOM
— P R E S S —

There is no Frigate like a Book
To take us Lands away,
Nor any Coursers like a Page
Of prancing Poetry —
This Traverse may the poorest take
Without oppress of Toll —
How frugal is the Chariot
That bears the Human soul.

— EMILY DICKINSON

"Some books are to be tasted,
others to be swallowed,
and some few to be chewed and digested..."

— FRANCIS BACON, *Essays*

TABLE of CONTENTS

INTRODUCTION................................PG VII

JOURNAL ENTRY PAGES................PGs 2-111

FEATURE LISTS............................PGs 113-159

New Words We Like! . . . . · PG 111
Our Favorite Quotes . . . . · PG 123
Most Memorable Characters. . . . PG 135
Most Surprising Story Twists. . . . PG 110
Books That Made Us Laugh . . . . · PG 111
Books That Made Us Cry. . . . . · PG 118
Books That Changed Us . . . . . · PG 152
Our Very Favorite Books! . . . . · PG 156

ADVENTURE QUESTS.......................PGs 161-185

World Explorers . . . . · PG 162
Time Travelers. . . . . · PG 161
Genre Hoppers . . . . · PG 166
The Serial Bookworm. . . . . . . · PG 168
The Literary Zookeeper. . . . . . · PG 169
High Adventure . . . . · PG 171
Myths & Legends . . . . · PG 173
Brainstormers . . . . · PG 175
Newbery Quest . . . . · PG 176
Caldecott Quest . . . . · PG 181

AUTHORS WE MET!.........................PGs 186-189

ABOUT THE CREATORS OF THIS JOURNAL..................PG 190

INTRODUCTION

by Douglas Kaine McKelvey

Consider the constellations.

The shapes we see in the night sky are but a fraction of the millions and billions and trillions of stars that are flung out there, burning and spinning in this vast universe.

If you were an astronomer, you might point your telescope in any direction and discover star after star after star. You might observe their patterns and discern the shapes they form together. But you would never find them all.

Not even close.

There are more stars out there than you could discover in a lifetime.

Or ten lifetimes.

Stories are like that too.

There are billions and trillions of stories out there.

Some are forever lost.

Some are old, or ancient and all but forgotten.

But there are also new stories unfolding all the time, everywhere, every day, swirling all around you, in the busy streets, in the quiet forests, in the memories and imaginations of every person.

Even your own life is a story. And you are a character in it.

But the thing about stories is this: Only a few of them ever get turned into books.

Only a few of them are ever fixed into words that can be read by others.

Most of them slip by without anyone even noticing that a story came and went and was lost forever.

That's why the stories that *do* get written into books matter so much to us.

Because those are the stories we can share and remember.

Those are the ones we can read and pass on to others.

Those are the stories that can shape us and change us and let us enter the lives of other people in other places and other times.

Those are the ones, out of all those trillions of stories in the vast story universe, that we can train the telescopes of our own imaginations upon. Those are the ones we can discover.

As you read stories, you'll be mapping out new constellations from the infinite story universe. Like an astronomer pointing a telescope here and there, discovering one star after another, you'll be discovering one story after another.

You'll be doing this for your whole life.

This book journal is like a travelogue then, a place where you can record all the stories you discover, so that even when you've read one hundred or two hundred or three hundred stories, you can always look back and remember them.

There's not just one right way to use this book journal. Look through the pages and consider the possibilities before you begin.

Most of the pages in your *Stories We Shared* journal are filled with spaces to write down book titles, and the names of authors and illustrators, and also to record your thoughts about the stories you read. There's even a little circle in the corner of each book entry. Use it however you want. For instance, you might use it to number the books you read, or to denote whether a book is a part of your library. So take a little while to consider how you want to use this book journal before you begin writing in it.

Towards the end of the book you'll find adventurous and challenging reading quests, and also special places to keep track of your favorite quotes and characters and even of new words you'll want to remember.

Become familiar with these lists before you begin to record your reading adventures in this journal, so you'll have them in mind as you journey.

In the pages of journal entries you'll also find some blank spaces for Notes & Doodles. You can use these however you want, but here are a few ideas:

Some people like to copy their favorite lines from the books they read.
Others use the blank spaces to draw characters and scenes from stories.
Or to write about how the story made them feel, or things it made them think about.
Or to list their favorite moment or character from a story.
Or to note the dates when they reread a favorite book.
Some people like to create a one sentence summary of each book they read, and write it in that space.

You and the people with whom you're sharing this journal can decide together what your own rules for those blank spaces will be.

The word *journal* comes from the same root word as the word *journey*. Both arise from the French root word *jour* which means *day*.
Journals and journeys always go together.
This journal will be the written record of your journey.
This journal will tell its own story.
Your story.
The story of your shared journey through a bright universe of stories.

So be bold. Taste. Explore. Discover. Go adventuring amongst the stories. Travel through time and space and see the world through the eyes of others who lived in times and places that in some ways are very different from your own, but that in other ways are so similar.

Map out a sky full of bright story constellations together.
Enjoy the journey. Enjoy the stories. Enjoy the hours spent together.

—Douglas Kaine McKelvey

JOURNAL ENTRIES
A place to keep track of all the books you read!

TITLE: _____

AUTHOR: _____

ILLUSTRATOR: _____

DATE FINISHED: _____ # PAGES: ___

STORY SHARED BY: _____

_____

DID WE LIKE IT? ☆ ☆ ☆ ☆ ☆

NOTES, DOODLES, ETC:

○

TITLE: _____

AUTHOR: _____

ILLUSTRATOR: _____

DATE FINISHED: _____ # PAGES: ___

STORY SHARED BY: _____

_____

DID WE LIKE IT? ☆ ☆ ☆ ☆ ☆

NOTES, DOODLES, ETC:

○

TITLE: _____

AUTHOR: _____

ILLUSTRATOR: _____

DATE FINISHED: _____ # PAGES: ___

STORY SHARED BY: _____

_____

DID WE LIKE IT? ☆ ☆ ☆ ☆ ☆

NOTES, DOODLES, ETC:

○

TITLE: _____

AUTHOR: _____

ILLUSTRATOR: _____

DATE FINISHED: _____ # PAGES: ___

STORY SHARED BY: _____

_____

DID WE LIKE IT? ☆ ☆ ☆ ☆ ☆

NOTES, DOODLES, ETC:

○

TITLE: _____
AUTHOR: _____
ILLUSTRATOR: _____
DATE FINISHED: _____ # PAGES: ____
STORY SHARED BY: _____
_____
DID WE LIKE IT?   ☆ ☆ ☆ ☆ ☆
NOTES, DOODLES, ETC:

"But how
could you live
and have no
story to tell?"

— Fyodor Dostoyevsky, **White Nights**

TITLE: _____
AUTHOR: _____
ILLUSTRATOR: _____
DATE FINISHED: _____ # PAGES: ____
STORY SHARED BY: _____
_____
DID WE LIKE IT?   ☆ ☆ ☆ ☆ ☆
NOTES, DOODLES, ETC:

TITLE: _____
AUTHOR: _____
ILLUSTRATOR: _____
DATE FINISHED: _____ # PAGES: ____
STORY SHARED BY: _____
_____
DID WE LIKE IT?   ☆ ☆ ☆ ☆ ☆
NOTES, DOODLES, ETC:

TITLE: _____
AUTHOR: _____
ILLUSTRATOR: _____
DATE FINISHED: _____ #PAGES: ___
STORY SHARED BY: _____

Did we like it?   ☆ ☆ ☆ ☆ ☆
NOTES, DOODLES, ETC:

○

TITLE: _____
AUTHOR: _____
ILLUSTRATOR: _____
DATE FINISHED: _____ #PAGES: ___
STORY SHARED BY: _____

Did we like it?   ☆ ☆ ☆ ☆ ☆
NOTES, DOODLES, ETC:

○

TITLE: _____
AUTHOR: _____
ILLUSTRATOR: _____
DATE FINISHED: _____ #PAGES: ___
STORY SHARED BY: _____

Did we like it?   ☆ ☆ ☆ ☆ ☆
NOTES, DOODLES, ETC:

○

TITLE: _____
AUTHOR: _____
ILLUSTRATOR: _____
DATE FINISHED: _____ #PAGES: ___
STORY SHARED BY: _____
_____
Did we like it? ☆ ☆ ☆ ☆ ☆
NOTES, DOODLES, ETC:

TITLE: _____
AUTHOR: _____
ILLUSTRATOR: _____
DATE FINISHED: _____ #PAGES: ___
STORY SHARED BY: _____
_____
Did we like it? ☆ ☆ ☆ ☆ ☆
NOTES, DOODLES, ETC:

TITLE: _____
AUTHOR: _____
ILLUSTRATOR: _____
DATE FINISHED: _____ #PAGES: ___
STORY SHARED BY: _____
_____
Did we like it? ☆ ☆ ☆ ☆ ☆
NOTES, DOODLES, ETC:

TITLE: _____
AUTHOR: _____
ILLUSTRATOR: _____
DATE FINISHED: _____ #PAGES: ___
STORY SHARED BY: _____
_____
Did we like it? ☆ ☆ ☆ ☆ ☆
NOTES, DOODLES, ETC:

TITLE: _____
AUTHOR: _____
ILLUSTRATOR: _____
DATE FINISHED: _____ # PAGES: ___
STORY SHARED BY: _____

_____

DID WE LIKE IT? ☆ ☆ ☆ ☆ ☆
NOTES, DOODLES, ETC:

"My library
isn't very extensive
but every book in it
is a friend."

— L. M. Montgomery, **Anne's House of Dreams**

TITLE: _____
AUTHOR: _____
ILLUSTRATOR: _____
DATE FINISHED: _____ # PAGES: ___
STORY SHARED BY: _____

_____

DID WE LIKE IT? ☆ ☆ ☆ ☆ ☆
NOTES, DOODLES, ETC:

TITLE: _____
AUTHOR: _____
ILLUSTRATOR: _____
DATE FINISHED: _____ # PAGES: ___
STORY SHARED BY: _____

_____

DID WE LIKE IT? ☆ ☆ ☆ ☆ ☆
NOTES, DOODLES, ETC:

TITLE: _____
AUTHOR: _____
ILLUSTRATOR: _____
DATE FINISHED: _____ #PAGES: ___
STORY SHARED BY: _____

Did we like it? ☆☆☆☆☆
NOTES, DOODLES, ETC:

TITLE: _____
AUTHOR: _____
ILLUSTRATOR: _____
DATE FINISHED: _____ #PAGES: ___
STORY SHARED BY: _____

Did we like it? ☆☆☆☆☆
NOTES, DOODLES, ETC:

TITLE: _____
AUTHOR: _____
ILLUSTRATOR: _____
DATE FINISHED: _____ #PAGES: ___
STORY SHARED BY: _____

Did we like it? ☆☆☆☆☆
NOTES, DOODLES, ETC:

TITLE: _____
AUTHOR: _____
ILLUSTRATOR: _____
DATE FINISHED: _____ #PAGES: ___
STORY SHARED BY: _____

Did we like it? ☆☆☆☆☆
NOTES, DOODLES, ETC:

TITLE: _____
AUTHOR: _____
ILLUSTRATOR: _____
DATE FINISHED: _____ #PAGES: ___
STORY SHARED BY: _____

_____

DID WE LIKE IT? ☆ ☆ ☆ ☆ ☆
NOTES, DOODLES, ETC:

◯

TITLE: _____
AUTHOR: _____
ILLUSTRATOR: _____
DATE FINISHED: _____ #PAGES: ___
STORY SHARED BY: _____

_____

DID WE LIKE IT? ☆ ☆ ☆ ☆ ☆
NOTES, DOODLES, ETC:

◯

TITLE: _____
AUTHOR: _____
ILLUSTRATOR: _____
DATE FINISHED: _____ #PAGES: ___
STORY SHARED BY: _____

_____

DID WE LIKE IT? ☆ ☆ ☆ ☆ ☆
NOTES, DOODLES, ETC:

◯

TITLE: _____
AUTHOR: _____
ILLUSTRATOR: _____
DATE FINISHED: _____ #PAGES: ___
STORY SHARED BY: _____

_____

DID WE LIKE IT? ☆ ☆ ☆ ☆ ☆
NOTES, DOODLES, ETC:

◯

TITLE: _____
AUTHOR: _____
ILLUSTRATOR: _____
DATE FINISHED: _____ #PAGES: ___
STORY SHARED BY: _____

Did we like it?   ☆ ☆ ☆ ☆ ☆
NOTES, DOODLES, ETC:

○

TITLE: _____
AUTHOR: _____
ILLUSTRATOR: _____
DATE FINISHED: _____ #PAGES: ___
STORY SHARED BY: _____

Did we like it?   ☆ ☆ ☆ ☆ ☆
NOTES, DOODLES, ETC:

○

"Once you
      learn to read,
   you will be
      forever free."

— Frederick Douglass

TITLE: _____
AUTHOR: _____
ILLUSTRATOR: _____
DATE FINISHED: _____ #PAGES: ___
STORY SHARED BY: _____

Did we like it?   ☆ ☆ ☆ ☆ ☆
NOTES, DOODLES, ETC:

○

TITLE: _____
AUTHOR: _____
ILLUSTRATOR: _____
DATE FINISHED: _____ # PAGES: ___
STORY SHARED BY: _____

DID WE LIKE IT?   ☆ ☆ ☆ ☆ ☆
NOTES, DOODLES, ETC:

○

TITLE: _____
AUTHOR: _____
ILLUSTRATOR: _____
DATE FINISHED: _____ # PAGES: ___
STORY SHARED BY: _____

DID WE LIKE IT?   ☆ ☆ ☆ ☆ ☆
NOTES, DOODLES, ETC:

○

TITLE: _____
AUTHOR: _____
ILLUSTRATOR: _____
DATE FINISHED: _____ # PAGES: ___
STORY SHARED BY: _____

DID WE LIKE IT?   ☆ ☆ ☆ ☆ ☆
NOTES, DOODLES, ETC:

○

TITLE: _____
AUTHOR: _____
ILLUSTRATOR: _____
DATE FINISHED: _____ # PAGES: ___
STORY SHARED BY: _____

DID WE LIKE IT?   ☆ ☆ ☆ ☆ ☆
NOTES, DOODLES, ETC:

○

TITLE: _____
AUTHOR: _____
ILLUSTRATOR: _____
DATE FINISHED: _____ #PAGES: ___
STORY SHARED BY: _____

Did we like it? ☆ ☆ ☆ ☆ ☆
NOTES, DOODLES, ETC:

○

TITLE: _____
AUTHOR: _____
ILLUSTRATOR: _____
DATE FINISHED: _____ #PAGES: ___
STORY SHARED BY: _____

Did we like it? ☆ ☆ ☆ ☆ ☆
NOTES, DOODLES, ETC:

○

TITLE: _____
AUTHOR: _____
ILLUSTRATOR: _____
DATE FINISHED: _____ #PAGES: ___
STORY SHARED BY: _____

Did we like it? ☆ ☆ ☆ ☆ ☆
NOTES, DOODLES, ETC:

○

"There are no
uninteresting
things,
only
uninterested
people."

— G. K. Chesterton, **Defendant**

TITLE:_____
AUTHOR:_____
ILLUSTRATOR:_____
DATE FINISHED:_____ #PAGES:___
STORY SHARED BY:_____

DID WE LIKE IT? ☆ ☆ ☆ ☆ ☆
NOTES, DOODLES, ETC:

TITLE:_____
AUTHOR:_____
ILLUSTRATOR:_____
DATE FINISHED:_____ #PAGES:___
STORY SHARED BY:_____

DID WE LIKE IT? ☆ ☆ ☆ ☆ ☆
NOTES, DOODLES, ETC:

TITLE:_____
AUTHOR:_____
ILLUSTRATOR:_____
DATE FINISHED:_____ #PAGES:___
STORY SHARED BY:_____

DID WE LIKE IT? ☆ ☆ ☆ ☆ ☆
NOTES, DOODLES, ETC:

TITLE: _____
AUTHOR: _____
ILLUSTRATOR: _____
DATE FINISHED: _____ #PAGES: ___
STORY SHARED BY: _____

_____

DID WE LIKE IT?   ☆ ☆ ☆ ☆ ☆
NOTES, DOODLES, ETC:

○

TITLE: _____
AUTHOR: _____
ILLUSTRATOR: _____
DATE FINISHED: _____ #PAGES: ___
STORY SHARED BY: _____

_____

DID WE LIKE IT?   ☆ ☆ ☆ ☆ ☆
NOTES, DOODLES, ETC:

○

TITLE: _____
AUTHOR: _____
ILLUSTRATOR: _____
DATE FINISHED: _____ #PAGES: ___
STORY SHARED BY: _____

_____

DID WE LIKE IT?   ☆ ☆ ☆ ☆ ☆
NOTES, DOODLES, ETC:

○

TITLE: _____
AUTHOR: _____
ILLUSTRATOR: _____
DATE FINISHED: _____ #PAGES: ___
STORY SHARED BY: _____

_____

DID WE LIKE IT?   ☆ ☆ ☆ ☆ ☆
NOTES, DOODLES, ETC:

○

TITLE: _____
AUTHOR: _____
ILLUSTRATOR: _____
DATE FINISHED: _____ # PAGES: ___
STORY SHARED BY: _____

Did we like it?   ☆ ☆ ☆ ☆ ☆
NOTES, DOODLES, ETC:

TITLE: _____
AUTHOR: _____
ILLUSTRATOR: _____
DATE FINISHED: _____ # PAGES: ___
STORY SHARED BY: _____

Did we like it?   ☆ ☆ ☆ ☆ ☆
NOTES, DOODLES, ETC:

TITLE: _____
AUTHOR: _____
ILLUSTRATOR: _____
DATE FINISHED: _____ # PAGES: ___
STORY SHARED BY: _____

Did we like it?   ☆ ☆ ☆ ☆ ☆
NOTES, DOODLES, ETC:

TITLE: _____
AUTHOR: _____
ILLUSTRATOR: _____
DATE FINISHED: _____ # PAGES: ___
STORY SHARED BY: _____

Did we like it?   ☆ ☆ ☆ ☆ ☆
NOTES, DOODLES, ETC:

TITLE: _____

AUTHOR: _____

ILLUSTRATOR: _____

DATE FINISHED: _____ #PAGES: ___

STORY SHARED BY: _____

_____

Did we like it?   ☆ ☆ ☆ ☆ ☆

NOTES, DOODLES, ETC:

○

TITLE: _____

AUTHOR: _____

ILLUSTRATOR: _____

DATE FINISHED: _____ #PAGES: ___

STORY SHARED BY: _____

_____

Did we like it?   ☆ ☆ ☆ ☆ ☆

NOTES, DOODLES, ETC:

○

TITLE: _____

AUTHOR: _____

ILLUSTRATOR: _____

DATE FINISHED: _____ #PAGES: ___

STORY SHARED BY: _____

_____

Did we like it?   ☆ ☆ ☆ ☆ ☆

NOTES, DOODLES, ETC:

○

TITLE: _____

AUTHOR: _____

ILLUSTRATOR: _____

DATE FINISHED: _____ #PAGES: ___

STORY SHARED BY: _____

_____

Did we like it?   ☆ ☆ ☆ ☆ ☆

NOTES, DOODLES, ETC:

○

TITLE: _____
AUTHOR: _____
ILLUSTRATOR: _____
DATE FINISHED: _____ #PAGES: ____
STORY SHARED BY: _____

Did we like it? ☆ ☆ ☆ ☆ ☆
NOTES, DOODLES, ETC:

○

TITLE: _____
AUTHOR: _____
ILLUSTRATOR: _____
DATE FINISHED: _____ #PAGES: ____
STORY SHARED BY: _____

Did we like it? ☆ ☆ ☆ ☆ ☆
NOTES, DOODLES, ETC:

○

TITLE: _____
AUTHOR: _____
ILLUSTRATOR: _____
DATE FINISHED: _____ #PAGES: ____
STORY SHARED BY: _____

Did we like it? ☆ ☆ ☆ ☆ ☆
NOTES, DOODLES, ETC:

○

TITLE: _____
AUTHOR: _____
ILLUSTRATOR: _____
DATE FINISHED: _____ #PAGES: ___
STORY SHARED BY: _____
_____
DID WE LIKE IT? ☆ ☆ ☆ ☆ ☆
NOTES, DOODLES, ETC:

○

TITLE: _____
AUTHOR: _____
ILLUSTRATOR: _____
DATE FINISHED: _____ #PAGES: ___
STORY SHARED BY: _____
_____
DID WE LIKE IT? ☆ ☆ ☆ ☆ ☆
NOTES, DOODLES, ETC:

○

TITLE: _____
AUTHOR: _____
ILLUSTRATOR: _____
DATE FINISHED: _____ #PAGES: ___
STORY SHARED BY: _____
_____
DID WE LIKE IT? ☆ ☆ ☆ ☆ ☆
NOTES, DOODLES, ETC:

○

TITLE: _____
AUTHOR: _____
ILLUSTRATOR: _____
DATE FINISHED: _____ #PAGES: ___
STORY SHARED BY: _____
_____
DID WE LIKE IT? ☆ ☆ ☆ ☆ ☆
NOTES, DOODLES, ETC:

○

TITLE: _____

AUTHOR: _____

ILLUSTRATOR: _____

DATE FINISHED: _____ # PAGES: ___

STORY SHARED BY: _____

DID WE LIKE IT? ☆ ☆ ☆ ☆ ☆

NOTES, DOODLES, ETC:

○

TITLE: _____

AUTHOR: _____

ILLUSTRATOR: _____

DATE FINISHED: _____ # PAGES: ___

STORY SHARED BY: _____

DID WE LIKE IT? ☆ ☆ ☆ ☆ ☆

NOTES, DOODLES, ETC:

○

TITLE: _____

AUTHOR: _____

ILLUSTRATOR: _____

DATE FINISHED: _____ # PAGES: ___

STORY SHARED BY: _____

DID WE LIKE IT? ☆ ☆ ☆ ☆ ☆

NOTES, DOODLES, ETC:

○

TITLE: _____

AUTHOR: _____

ILLUSTRATOR: _____

DATE FINISHED: _____ # PAGES: ___

STORY SHARED BY: _____

DID WE LIKE IT? ☆ ☆ ☆ ☆ ☆

NOTES, DOODLES, ETC:

○

> "All I have learned,
> I learned
> from books."
>
> — Abraham Lincoln

TITLE: _____

AUTHOR: _____

ILLUSTRATOR: _____

DATE FINISHED: _____ #PAGES: ___

STORY SHARED BY: _____

Did we like it? ☆ ☆ ☆ ☆ ☆

NOTES, DOODLES, ETC:

○

TITLE: _____

AUTHOR: _____

ILLUSTRATOR: _____

DATE FINISHED: _____ #PAGES: ___

STORY SHARED BY: _____

Did we like it? ☆ ☆ ☆ ☆ ☆

NOTES, DOODLES, ETC:

○

TITLE: _____

AUTHOR: _____

ILLUSTRATOR: _____

DATE FINISHED: _____ #PAGES: ___

STORY SHARED BY: _____

Did we like it? ☆ ☆ ☆ ☆ ☆

NOTES, DOODLES, ETC:

○

TITLE: _____
AUTHOR: _____
ILLUSTRATOR: _____
DATE FINISHED: _____ # PAGES: ___
STORY SHARED BY: _____

DID WE LIKE IT?   ☆ ☆ ☆ ☆ ☆
NOTES, DOODLES, ETC:

○

TITLE: _____
AUTHOR: _____
ILLUSTRATOR: _____
DATE FINISHED: _____ # PAGES: ___
STORY SHARED BY: _____

DID WE LIKE IT?   ☆ ☆ ☆ ☆ ☆
NOTES, DOODLES, ETC:

○

"A book is like
a garden,
carried in
the pocket."

— Chinese Proverb

TITLE: _____
AUTHOR: _____
ILLUSTRATOR: _____
DATE FINISHED: _____ # PAGES: ___
STORY SHARED BY: _____

DID WE LIKE IT?   ☆ ☆ ☆ ☆ ☆
NOTES, DOODLES, ETC:

○

TITLE: _____

AUTHOR: _____

ILLUSTRATOR: _____

DATE FINISHED: _____ #PAGES: ___

STORY SHARED BY: _____

_____

DID WE LIKE IT? ☆ ☆ ☆ ☆ ☆

NOTES, DOODLES, ETC:

○

TITLE: _____

AUTHOR: _____

ILLUSTRATOR: _____

DATE FINISHED: _____ #PAGES: ___

STORY SHARED BY: _____

_____

DID WE LIKE IT? ☆ ☆ ☆ ☆ ☆

NOTES, DOODLES, ETC:

○

TITLE: _____

AUTHOR: _____

ILLUSTRATOR: _____

DATE FINISHED: _____ #PAGES: ___

STORY SHARED BY: _____

_____

DID WE LIKE IT? ☆ ☆ ☆ ☆ ☆

NOTES, DOODLES, ETC:

○

TITLE: _____

AUTHOR: _____

ILLUSTRATOR: _____

DATE FINISHED: _____ #PAGES: ___

STORY SHARED BY: _____

_____

DID WE LIKE IT? ☆ ☆ ☆ ☆ ☆

NOTES, DOODLES, ETC:

○

TITLE: _____
AUTHOR: _____
ILLUSTRATOR: _____
DATE FINISHED: _____ #PAGES: ___
STORY SHARED BY: _____

Did we like it? ☆ ☆ ☆ ☆ ☆
NOTES, DOODLES, ETC:

○

TITLE: _____
AUTHOR: _____
ILLUSTRATOR: _____
DATE FINISHED: _____ #PAGES: ___
STORY SHARED BY: _____

Did we like it? ☆ ☆ ☆ ☆ ☆
NOTES, DOODLES, ETC:

○

TITLE: _____
AUTHOR: _____
ILLUSTRATOR: _____
DATE FINISHED: _____ #PAGES: ___
STORY SHARED BY: _____

Did we like it? ☆ ☆ ☆ ☆ ☆
NOTES, DOODLES, ETC:

○

TITLE: _____
AUTHOR: _____
ILLUSTRATOR: _____
DATE FINISHED: _____ #PAGES: ___
STORY SHARED BY: _____

Did we like it? ☆ ☆ ☆ ☆ ☆
NOTES, DOODLES, ETC:

○

TITLE: _____
AUTHOR: _____
ILLUSTRATOR: _____
DATE FINISHED: _____ # PAGES: ___
STORY SHARED BY: _____
_____
DID WE LIKE IT? ☆ ☆ ☆ ☆ ☆
NOTES, DOODLES, ETC:

TITLE: _____
AUTHOR: _____
ILLUSTRATOR: _____
DATE FINISHED: _____ # PAGES: ___
STORY SHARED BY: _____
_____
DID WE LIKE IT? ☆ ☆ ☆ ☆ ☆
NOTES, DOODLES, ETC:

TITLE: _____
AUTHOR: _____
ILLUSTRATOR: _____
DATE FINISHED: _____ # PAGES: ___
STORY SHARED BY: _____
_____
DID WE LIKE IT? ☆ ☆ ☆ ☆ ☆
NOTES, DOODLES, ETC:

TITLE: _____
AUTHOR: _____
ILLUSTRATOR: _____
DATE FINISHED: _____ # PAGES: ___
STORY SHARED BY: _____
_____
DID WE LIKE IT? ☆ ☆ ☆ ☆ ☆
NOTES, DOODLES, ETC:

TITLE: _____
AUTHOR: _____
ILLUSTRATOR: _____
DATE FINISHED: _____ #PAGES: ___
STORY SHARED BY: _____
_____

DID WE LIKE IT? ☆ ☆ ☆ ☆ ☆
NOTES, DOODLES, ETC:

TITLE: _____
AUTHOR: _____
ILLUSTRATOR: _____
DATE FINISHED: _____ #PAGES: ___
STORY SHARED BY: _____
_____

DID WE LIKE IT? ☆ ☆ ☆ ☆ ☆
NOTES, DOODLES, ETC:

TITLE: _____
AUTHOR: _____
ILLUSTRATOR: _____
DATE FINISHED: _____ #PAGES: ___
STORY SHARED BY: _____

DID WE LIKE IT? ☆ ☆ ☆ ☆ ☆
NOTES, DOODLES, ETC:

TITLE: _____
AUTHOR: _____
ILLUSTRATOR: _____
DATE FINISHED: _____ #PAGES: ___
STORY SHARED BY: _____

DID WE LIKE IT? ☆ ☆ ☆ ☆ ☆
NOTES, DOODLES, ETC:

TITLE: _____

AUTHOR: _____

ILLUSTRATOR: _____

DATE FINISHED: _____ # PAGES: ___

STORY SHARED BY: _____

_____

DID WE LIKE IT?   ☆ ☆ ☆ ☆ ☆

NOTES, DOODLES, ETC:

TITLE: _____

AUTHOR: _____

ILLUSTRATOR: _____

DATE FINISHED: _____ # PAGES: ___

STORY SHARED BY: _____

_____

DID WE LIKE IT?   ☆ ☆ ☆ ☆ ☆

NOTES, DOODLES, ETC:

TITLE: _____

AUTHOR: _____

ILLUSTRATOR: _____

DATE FINISHED: _____ # PAGES: ___

STORY SHARED BY: _____

_____

DID WE LIKE IT?   ☆ ☆ ☆ ☆ ☆

NOTES, DOODLES, ETC:

TITLE: _____
AUTHOR: _____
ILLUSTRATOR: _____
DATE FINISHED: _____ # PAGES: ___
STORY SHARED BY: _____

_____

DID WE LIKE IT?   ☆ ☆ ☆ ☆ ☆
NOTES, DOODLES, ETC:

◯

"My task
which I am
trying to achieve is,
by the power of
the written word,
to make you hear,
to make you feel—
it is,
before all,
to make you see."

— Joseph Conrad, **Lord Jim**

TITLE: _____
AUTHOR: _____
ILLUSTRATOR: _____
DATE FINISHED: _____ # PAGES: ___
STORY SHARED BY: _____

_____

DID WE LIKE IT?   ☆ ☆ ☆ ☆ ☆
NOTES, DOODLES, ETC:

◯

TITLE: _____
AUTHOR: _____
ILLUSTRATOR: _____
DATE FINISHED: _____ # PAGES: ___
STORY SHARED BY: _____

_____

DID WE LIKE IT?   ☆ ☆ ☆ ☆ ☆
NOTES, DOODLES, ETC:

◯

TITLE: _____
AUTHOR: _____
ILLUSTRATOR: _____
DATE FINISHED: _____   # PAGES: ___
STORY SHARED BY: _____
_____
DID WE LIKE IT?   ☆ ☆ ☆ ☆ ☆
NOTES, DOODLES, ETC:

TITLE: _____
AUTHOR: _____
ILLUSTRATOR: _____
DATE FINISHED: _____   # PAGES: ___
STORY SHARED BY: _____
_____
DID WE LIKE IT?   ☆ ☆ ☆ ☆ ☆
NOTES, DOODLES, ETC:

TITLE: _____
AUTHOR: _____
ILLUSTRATOR: _____
DATE FINISHED: _____   # PAGES: ___
STORY SHARED BY: _____
_____
DID WE LIKE IT?   ☆ ☆ ☆ ☆ ☆
NOTES, DOODLES, ETC:

TITLE: _____
AUTHOR: _____
ILLUSTRATOR: _____
DATE FINISHED: _____   # PAGES: ___
STORY SHARED BY: _____
_____
DID WE LIKE IT?   ☆ ☆ ☆ ☆ ☆
NOTES, DOODLES, ETC:

TITLE: _____
AUTHOR: _____
ILLUSTRATOR: _____
DATE FINISHED: _____ # PAGES: ___
STORY SHARED BY: _____
_____

DID WE LIKE IT? ☆ ☆ ☆ ☆ ☆
NOTES, DOODLES, ETC:

○

TITLE: _____
AUTHOR: _____
ILLUSTRATOR: _____
DATE FINISHED: _____ # PAGES: ___
STORY SHARED BY: _____
_____

DID WE LIKE IT? ☆ ☆ ☆ ☆ ☆
NOTES, DOODLES, ETC:

○

TITLE: _____
AUTHOR: _____
ILLUSTRATOR: _____
DATE FINISHED: _____ # PAGES: ___
STORY SHARED BY: _____

DID WE LIKE IT? ☆ ☆ ☆ ☆ ☆
NOTES, DOODLES, ETC:

○

TITLE: _____
AUTHOR: _____
ILLUSTRATOR: _____
DATE FINISHED: _____ # PAGES: ___
STORY SHARED BY: _____

DID WE LIKE IT? ☆ ☆ ☆ ☆ ☆
NOTES, DOODLES, ETC:

○

TITLE: _____
AUTHOR: _____
ILLUSTRATOR: _____
DATE FINISHED: _____ # PAGES: ___
STORY SHARED BY: _____

Did we like it?   ☆ ☆ ☆ ☆ ☆
NOTES, DOODLES, ETC:

TITLE: _____
AUTHOR: _____
ILLUSTRATOR: _____
DATE FINISHED: _____ # PAGES: ___
STORY SHARED BY: _____

Did we like it?   ☆ ☆ ☆ ☆ ☆
NOTES, DOODLES, ETC:

TITLE: _____
AUTHOR: _____
ILLUSTRATOR: _____
DATE FINISHED: _____ # PAGES: ___
STORY SHARED BY: _____

Did we like it?   ☆ ☆ ☆ ☆ ☆
NOTES, DOODLES, ETC:

Title: _____
Author: _____
Illustrator: _____
Date finished: _____ #Pages: ___
Story shared by: _____

Did we like it? ☆ ☆ ☆ ☆ ☆
Notes, doodles, etc:

○

Title: _____
Author: _____
Illustrator: _____
Date finished: _____ #Pages: ___
Story shared by: _____

Did we like it? ☆ ☆ ☆ ☆ ☆
Notes, doodles, etc:

○

Title: _____
Author: _____
Illustrator: _____
Date finished: _____ #Pages: ___
Story shared by: _____

Did we like it? ☆ ☆ ☆ ☆ ☆
Notes, doodles, etc:

○

Title: _____
Author: _____
Illustrator: _____
Date finished: _____ #Pages: ___
Story shared by: _____

Did we like it? ☆ ☆ ☆ ☆ ☆
Notes, doodles, etc:

○

TITLE: _____

AUTHOR: _____

ILLUSTRATOR: _____

DATE FINISHED: _____ # PAGES: ___

STORY SHARED BY: _____

DID WE LIKE IT? ☆ ☆ ☆ ☆ ☆

NOTES, DOODLES, ETC:

◯

TITLE: _____

AUTHOR: _____

ILLUSTRATOR: _____

DATE FINISHED: _____ # PAGES: ___

STORY SHARED BY: _____

DID WE LIKE IT? ☆ ☆ ☆ ☆ ☆

NOTES, DOODLES, ETC:

◯

TITLE: _____

AUTHOR: _____

ILLUSTRATOR: _____

DATE FINISHED: _____ # PAGES: ___

STORY SHARED BY: _____

DID WE LIKE IT? ☆ ☆ ☆ ☆ ☆

NOTES, DOODLES, ETC:

◯

TITLE: _____

AUTHOR: _____

ILLUSTRATOR: _____

DATE FINISHED: _____ # PAGES: ___

STORY SHARED BY: _____

DID WE LIKE IT? ☆ ☆ ☆ ☆ ☆

NOTES, DOODLES, ETC:

◯

TITLE: _____
AUTHOR: _____
ILLUSTRATOR: _____
DATE FINISHED: _____ # PAGES: ____
STORY SHARED BY: _____

DID WE LIKE IT? ☆ ☆ ☆ ☆ ☆
NOTES, DOODLES, ETC:

○

TITLE: _____
AUTHOR: _____
ILLUSTRATOR: _____
DATE FINISHED: _____ # PAGES: ____
STORY SHARED BY: _____

DID WE LIKE IT? ☆ ☆ ☆ ☆ ☆
NOTES, DOODLES, ETC:

○

TITLE: _____
AUTHOR: _____
ILLUSTRATOR: _____
DATE FINISHED: _____ # PAGES: ____
STORY SHARED BY: _____

DID WE LIKE IT? ☆ ☆ ☆ ☆ ☆
NOTES, DOODLES, ETC:

○

"It is never too late to be wise."

— Daniel Defoe, **Robinson Crusoe**

TITLE: _____
AUTHOR: _____
ILLUSTRATOR: _____
DATE FINISHED: _____ #PAGES: ___
STORY SHARED BY: _____

Did we like it? ☆ ☆ ☆ ☆ ☆
NOTES, DOODLES, ETC:

TITLE: _____
AUTHOR: _____
ILLUSTRATOR: _____
DATE FINISHED: _____ #PAGES: ___
STORY SHARED BY: _____

Did we like it? ☆ ☆ ☆ ☆ ☆
NOTES, DOODLES, ETC:

TITLE: _____
AUTHOR: _____
ILLUSTRATOR: _____
DATE FINISHED: _____ #PAGES: ___
STORY SHARED BY: _____

Did we like it? ☆ ☆ ☆ ☆ ☆
NOTES, DOODLES, ETC:

TITLE: _____
AUTHOR: _____
ILLUSTRATOR: _____
DATE FINISHED: _____ #PAGES: ___
STORY SHARED BY: _____

Did we like it? ☆ ☆ ☆ ☆ ☆
NOTES, DOODLES, ETC:

TITLE: _____

AUTHOR: _____

ILLUSTRATOR: _____

DATE FINISHED: _____ # PAGES: ___

STORY SHARED BY: _____

_____

DID WE LIKE IT?   ☆ ☆ ☆ ☆ ☆

NOTES, DOODLES, ETC:

TITLE: _____

AUTHOR: _____

ILLUSTRATOR: _____

DATE FINISHED: _____ # PAGES: ___

STORY SHARED BY: _____

_____

DID WE LIKE IT?   ☆ ☆ ☆ ☆ ☆

NOTES, DOODLES, ETC:

TITLE: _____

AUTHOR: _____

ILLUSTRATOR: _____

DATE FINISHED: _____ # PAGES: ___

STORY SHARED BY: _____

_____

DID WE LIKE IT?   ☆ ☆ ☆ ☆ ☆

NOTES, DOODLES, ETC:

TITLE: _____

AUTHOR: _____

ILLUSTRATOR: _____

DATE FINISHED: _____ # PAGES: ___

STORY SHARED BY: _____

_____

DID WE LIKE IT?   ☆ ☆ ☆ ☆ ☆

NOTES, DOODLES, ETC:

> "A love for
> good books
> [is] one of the best
> safeguards
> a man
> could have."
>
> — Louisa May Alcott, **Eight Cousins**

TITLE: _____
AUTHOR: _____
ILLUSTRATOR: _____
DATE FINISHED: _____ #PAGES:___
STORY SHARED BY: _____
_____

DID WE LIKE IT? ☆ ☆ ☆ ☆ ☆
NOTES, DOODLES, ETC:

TITLE: _____
AUTHOR: _____
ILLUSTRATOR: _____
DATE FINISHED: _____ #PAGES:___
STORY SHARED BY: _____
_____

DID WE LIKE IT? ☆ ☆ ☆ ☆ ☆
NOTES, DOODLES, ETC:

TITLE: _____
AUTHOR: _____
ILLUSTRATOR: _____
DATE FINISHED: _____ #PAGES:___
STORY SHARED BY: _____
_____

DID WE LIKE IT? ☆ ☆ ☆ ☆ ☆
NOTES, DOODLES, ETC:

TITLE: _____
AUTHOR: _____
ILLUSTRATOR: _____
DATE FINISHED: _____ #PAGES: ___
STORY SHARED BY: _____

DID WE LIKE IT?   ☆ ☆ ☆ ☆ ☆
NOTES, DOODLES, ETC:

TITLE: _____
AUTHOR: _____
ILLUSTRATOR: _____
DATE FINISHED: _____ #PAGES: ___
STORY SHARED BY: _____

DID WE LIKE IT?   ☆ ☆ ☆ ☆ ☆
NOTES, DOODLES, ETC:

TITLE: _____
AUTHOR: _____
ILLUSTRATOR: _____
DATE FINISHED: _____ #PAGES: ___
STORY SHARED BY: _____

DID WE LIKE IT?   ☆ ☆ ☆ ☆ ☆
NOTES, DOODLES, ETC:

TITLE: _____
AUTHOR: _____
ILLUSTRATOR: _____
DATE FINISHED: _____ #PAGES: ___
STORY SHARED BY: _____

DID WE LIKE IT?   ☆ ☆ ☆ ☆ ☆
NOTES, DOODLES, ETC:

TITLE: _____

AUTHOR: _____

ILLUSTRATOR: _____

DATE FINISHED: _____ # PAGES: ____

STORY SHARED BY: _____

_____

DID WE LIKE IT? ☆ ☆ ☆ ☆ ☆

NOTES, DOODLES, ETC:

○

TITLE: _____

AUTHOR: _____

ILLUSTRATOR: _____

DATE FINISHED: _____ # PAGES: ____

STORY SHARED BY: _____

_____

DID WE LIKE IT? ☆ ☆ ☆ ☆ ☆

NOTES, DOODLES, ETC:

○

TITLE: _____

AUTHOR: _____

ILLUSTRATOR: _____

DATE FINISHED: _____ # PAGES: ____

STORY SHARED BY: _____

_____

DID WE LIKE IT? ☆ ☆ ☆ ☆ ☆

NOTES, DOODLES, ETC:

○

TITLE: _____

AUTHOR: _____

ILLUSTRATOR: _____

DATE FINISHED: _____ # PAGES: ____

STORY SHARED BY: _____

_____

DID WE LIKE IT? ☆ ☆ ☆ ☆ ☆

NOTES, DOODLES, ETC:

○

TITLE: _____

AUTHOR: _____

ILLUSTRATOR: _____

DATE FINISHED: _____ #PAGES: ___

STORY SHARED BY: _____

_____

DID WE LIKE IT?   ☆ ☆ ☆ ☆ ☆

NOTES, DOODLES, ETC:

○

TITLE: _____

AUTHOR: _____

ILLUSTRATOR: _____

DATE FINISHED: _____ #PAGES: ___

STORY SHARED BY: _____

_____

DID WE LIKE IT?   ☆ ☆ ☆ ☆ ☆

NOTES, DOODLES, ETC:

○

TITLE: _____

AUTHOR: _____

ILLUSTRATOR: _____

DATE FINISHED: _____ #PAGES: ___

STORY SHARED BY: _____

_____

DID WE LIKE IT?   ☆ ☆ ☆ ☆ ☆

NOTES, DOODLES, ETC:

○

TITLE: _____

AUTHOR: _____

ILLUSTRATOR: _____

DATE FINISHED: _____ #PAGES: ___

STORY SHARED BY: _____

_____

DID WE LIKE IT?   ☆ ☆ ☆ ☆ ☆

NOTES, DOODLES, ETC:

○

TITLE: _____
AUTHOR: _____
ILLUSTRATOR: _____
DATE FINISHED: _____ #PAGES: ___
STORY SHARED BY: _____
_____
DID WE LIKE IT?   ☆ ☆ ☆ ☆ ☆
NOTES, DOODLES, ETC:

TITLE: _____
AUTHOR: _____
ILLUSTRATOR: _____
DATE FINISHED: _____ #PAGES: ___
STORY SHARED BY: _____
_____
DID WE LIKE IT?   ☆ ☆ ☆ ☆ ☆
NOTES, DOODLES, ETC:

TITLE: _____
AUTHOR: _____
ILLUSTRATOR: _____
DATE FINISHED: _____ #PAGES: ___
STORY SHARED BY: _____
_____
DID WE LIKE IT?   ☆ ☆ ☆ ☆ ☆
NOTES, DOODLES, ETC:

TITLE: _____

AUTHOR: _____

ILLUSTRATOR: _____

DATE FINISHED: _____ #PAGES: ___

STORY SHARED BY: _____

Did we like it?   ☆ ☆ ☆ ☆ ☆

NOTES, DOODLES, ETC:

○

TITLE: _____

AUTHOR: _____

ILLUSTRATOR: _____

DATE FINISHED: _____ #PAGES: ___

STORY SHARED BY: _____

Did we like it?   ☆ ☆ ☆ ☆ ☆

NOTES, DOODLES, ETC:

○

TITLE: _____

AUTHOR: _____

ILLUSTRATOR: _____

DATE FINISHED: _____ #PAGES: ___

STORY SHARED BY: _____

Did we like it?   ☆ ☆ ☆ ☆ ☆

NOTES, DOODLES, ETC:

○

TITLE: _____

AUTHOR: _____

ILLUSTRATOR: _____

DATE FINISHED: _____ #PAGES: ___

STORY SHARED BY: _____

Did we like it?   ☆ ☆ ☆ ☆ ☆

NOTES, DOODLES, ETC:

○

TITLE: _____

AUTHOR: _____

ILLUSTRATOR: _____

DATE FINISHED: _____ # PAGES: ___

STORY SHARED BY: _____

Did we like it? ☆ ☆ ☆ ☆ ☆

NOTES, DOODLES, ETC:

○

TITLE: _____

AUTHOR: _____

ILLUSTRATOR: _____

DATE FINISHED: _____ # PAGES: ___

STORY SHARED BY: _____

Did we like it? ☆ ☆ ☆ ☆ ☆

NOTES, DOODLES, ETC:

○

TITLE: _____

AUTHOR: _____

ILLUSTRATOR: _____

DATE FINISHED: _____ # PAGES: ___

STORY SHARED BY: _____

Did we like it? ☆ ☆ ☆ ☆ ☆

NOTES, DOODLES, ETC:

○

TITLE: _____

AUTHOR: _____

ILLUSTRATOR: _____

DATE FINISHED: _____ # PAGES: ___

STORY SHARED BY: _____

Did we like it? ☆ ☆ ☆ ☆ ☆

NOTES, DOODLES, ETC:

○

TITLE: _____

AUTHOR: _____

ILLUSTRATOR: _____

DATE FINISHED: _____ # PAGES: ____

STORY SHARED BY: _____

_____

DID WE LIKE IT? ☆ ☆ ☆ ☆ ☆

NOTES, DOODLES, ETC:

TITLE: _____

AUTHOR: _____

ILLUSTRATOR: _____

DATE FINISHED: _____ # PAGES: ____

STORY SHARED BY: _____

_____

DID WE LIKE IT? ☆ ☆ ☆ ☆ ☆

NOTES, DOODLES, ETC:

"A hero is
no braver than
an ordinary man,
but he is brave
five minutes
longer."

— Ralph Waldo Emerson

TITLE: _____

AUTHOR: _____

ILLUSTRATOR: _____

DATE FINISHED: _____ # PAGES: ____

STORY SHARED BY: _____

_____

DID WE LIKE IT? ☆ ☆ ☆ ☆ ☆

NOTES, DOODLES, ETC:

TITLE: _____

AUTHOR: _____

ILLUSTRATOR: _____

DATE FINISHED: _____ #PAGES: ___

STORY SHARED BY: _____

Did we like it? ☆ ☆ ☆ ☆ ☆

NOTES, DOODLES, ETC:

TITLE: _____

AUTHOR: _____

ILLUSTRATOR: _____

DATE FINISHED: _____ #PAGES: ___

STORY SHARED BY: _____

Did we like it? ☆ ☆ ☆ ☆ ☆

NOTES, DOODLES, ETC:

TITLE: _____

AUTHOR: _____

ILLUSTRATOR: _____

DATE FINISHED: _____ #PAGES: ___

STORY SHARED BY: _____

Did we like it? ☆ ☆ ☆ ☆ ☆

NOTES, DOODLES, ETC:

TITLE: _____

AUTHOR: _____

ILLUSTRATOR: _____

DATE FINISHED: _____ #PAGES: ___

STORY SHARED BY: _____

Did we like it? ☆ ☆ ☆ ☆ ☆

NOTES, DOODLES, ETC:

TITLE: _____
AUTHOR: _____
ILLUSTRATOR: _____
DATE FINISHED: _____ #PAGES: ___
STORY SHARED BY: _____
_____
DID WE LIKE IT?   ☆ ☆ ☆ ☆ ☆
NOTES, DOODLES, ETC:

○

TITLE: _____
AUTHOR: _____
ILLUSTRATOR: _____
DATE FINISHED: _____ #PAGES: ___
STORY SHARED BY: _____
_____
DID WE LIKE IT?   ☆ ☆ ☆ ☆ ☆
NOTES, DOODLES, ETC:

○

TITLE: _____
AUTHOR: _____
ILLUSTRATOR: _____
DATE FINISHED: _____ #PAGES: ___
STORY SHARED BY: _____
_____
DID WE LIKE IT?   ☆ ☆ ☆ ☆ ☆
NOTES, DOODLES, ETC:

○

TITLE: _____
AUTHOR: _____
ILLUSTRATOR: _____
DATE FINISHED: _____ #PAGES: ___
STORY SHARED BY: _____
_____
DID WE LIKE IT?   ☆ ☆ ☆ ☆ ☆
NOTES, DOODLES, ETC:

○

TITLE: _____
AUTHOR: _____
ILLUSTRATOR: _____
DATE FINISHED: _____ #PAGES: ___
STORY SHARED BY: _____

DID WE LIKE IT?   ☆ ☆ ☆ ☆ ☆
NOTES, DOODLES, ETC:

TITLE: _____
AUTHOR: _____
ILLUSTRATOR: _____
DATE FINISHED: _____ #PAGES: ___
STORY SHARED BY: _____

DID WE LIKE IT?   ☆ ☆ ☆ ☆ ☆
NOTES, DOODLES, ETC:

TITLE: _____
AUTHOR: _____
ILLUSTRATOR: _____
DATE FINISHED: _____ #PAGES: ___
STORY SHARED BY: _____

DID WE LIKE IT?   ☆ ☆ ☆ ☆ ☆
NOTES, DOODLES, ETC:

TITLE: _____
AUTHOR: _____
ILLUSTRATOR: _____
DATE FINISHED: _____ #PAGES: ___
STORY SHARED BY: _____

DID WE LIKE IT?   ☆ ☆ ☆ ☆ ☆
NOTES, DOODLES, ETC:

TITLE: _____
AUTHOR: _____
ILLUSTRATOR: _____
DATE FINISHED: _____ #PAGES: ___
STORY SHARED BY: _____

Did we like it? ☆ ☆ ☆ ☆ ☆
NOTES, DOODLES, ETC:

○

TITLE: _____
AUTHOR: _____
ILLUSTRATOR: _____
DATE FINISHED: _____ #PAGES: ___
STORY SHARED BY: _____

Did we like it? ☆ ☆ ☆ ☆ ☆
NOTES, DOODLES, ETC:

○

TITLE: _____
AUTHOR: _____
ILLUSTRATOR: _____
DATE FINISHED: _____ #PAGES: ___
STORY SHARED BY: _____

Did we like it? ☆ ☆ ☆ ☆ ☆
NOTES, DOODLES, ETC:

○

TITLE: _____
AUTHOR: _____
ILLUSTRATOR: _____
DATE FINISHED: _____ #PAGES: ___
STORY SHARED BY: _____

Did we like it? ☆ ☆ ☆ ☆ ☆
NOTES, DOODLES, ETC:

○

TITLE: _____
AUTHOR: _____
ILLUSTRATOR: _____
DATE FINISHED: _____ # PAGES: ___
STORY SHARED BY: _____

Did we like it? ☆ ☆ ☆ ☆ ☆
NOTES, DOODLES, ETC:

"The world calls them
its singers
and poets
and artists
and story-tellers;
but they are
just people
who have
never forgotten
the way to fairyland."

— L. M. Montgomery, **The Story Girl**

TITLE: _____
AUTHOR: _____
ILLUSTRATOR: _____
DATE FINISHED: _____ # PAGES: ___
STORY SHARED BY: _____

Did we like it? ☆ ☆ ☆ ☆ ☆
NOTES, DOODLES, ETC:

TITLE: _____
AUTHOR: _____
ILLUSTRATOR: _____
DATE FINISHED: _____ # PAGES: ___
STORY SHARED BY: _____

Did we like it? ☆ ☆ ☆ ☆ ☆
NOTES, DOODLES, ETC:

TITLE: _____

AUTHOR: _____

ILLUSTRATOR: _____

DATE FINISHED: _____ #PAGES: ____

STORY SHARED BY: _____

DID WE LIKE IT? ☆ ☆ ☆ ☆ ☆

NOTES, DOODLES, ETC:

TITLE: _____

AUTHOR: _____

ILLUSTRATOR: _____

DATE FINISHED: _____ #PAGES: ____

STORY SHARED BY: _____

DID WE LIKE IT? ☆ ☆ ☆ ☆ ☆

NOTES, DOODLES, ETC:

TITLE: _____

AUTHOR: _____

ILLUSTRATOR: _____

DATE FINISHED: _____ #PAGES: ____

STORY SHARED BY: _____

DID WE LIKE IT? ☆ ☆ ☆ ☆ ☆

NOTES, DOODLES, ETC:

TITLE: _____

AUTHOR: _____

ILLUSTRATOR: _____

DATE FINISHED: _____ #PAGES: ____

STORY SHARED BY: _____

DID WE LIKE IT? ☆ ☆ ☆ ☆ ☆

NOTES, DOODLES, ETC:

TITLE: _____
AUTHOR: _____
ILLUSTRATOR: _____
DATE FINISHED: _____ #PAGES: ___
STORY SHARED BY: _____

DID WE LIKE IT? ☆ ☆ ☆ ☆ ☆
NOTES, DOODLES, ETC:

○

TITLE: _____
AUTHOR: _____
ILLUSTRATOR: _____
DATE FINISHED: _____ #PAGES: ___
STORY SHARED BY: _____

DID WE LIKE IT? ☆ ☆ ☆ ☆ ☆
NOTES, DOODLES, ETC:

○

"An inconvenience
   is only an adventure
      wrongly considered;
   an adventure
      is an inconvenience
         rightly considered."

— G. K. Chesterton, **On Running After One's Hat**

TITLE: _____
AUTHOR: _____
ILLUSTRATOR: _____
DATE FINISHED: _____ #PAGES: ___
STORY SHARED BY: _____

DID WE LIKE IT? ☆ ☆ ☆ ☆ ☆
NOTES, DOODLES, ETC:

○

TITLE: _____

AUTHOR: _____

ILLUSTRATOR: _____

DATE FINISHED: _____ #PAGES: ___

STORY SHARED BY: _____

_____

DID WE LIKE IT? ☆ ☆ ☆ ☆ ☆

NOTES, DOODLES, ETC:

○

TITLE: _____

AUTHOR: _____

ILLUSTRATOR: _____

DATE FINISHED: _____ #PAGES: ___

STORY SHARED BY: _____

_____

DID WE LIKE IT? ☆ ☆ ☆ ☆ ☆

NOTES, DOODLES, ETC:

○

TITLE: _____

AUTHOR: _____

ILLUSTRATOR: _____

DATE FINISHED: _____ #PAGES: ___

STORY SHARED BY: _____

_____

DID WE LIKE IT? ☆ ☆ ☆ ☆ ☆

NOTES, DOODLES, ETC:

○

TITLE: _____

AUTHOR: _____

ILLUSTRATOR: _____

DATE FINISHED: _____ #PAGES: ___

STORY SHARED BY: _____

_____

DID WE LIKE IT? ☆ ☆ ☆ ☆ ☆

NOTES, DOODLES, ETC:

○

TITLE: _____

AUTHOR: _____

ILLUSTRATOR: _____

DATE FINISHED: _____ #PAGES: ___

STORY SHARED BY: _____

_____

DID WE LIKE IT? ☆ ☆ ☆ ☆ ☆

NOTES, DOODLES, ETC:

○

TITLE: _____

AUTHOR: _____

ILLUSTRATOR: _____

DATE FINISHED: _____ #PAGES: ___

STORY SHARED BY: _____

_____

DID WE LIKE IT? ☆ ☆ ☆ ☆ ☆

NOTES, DOODLES, ETC:

○

TITLE: _____

AUTHOR: _____

ILLUSTRATOR: _____

DATE FINISHED: _____ #PAGES: ___

STORY SHARED BY: _____

_____

DID WE LIKE IT? ☆ ☆ ☆ ☆ ☆

NOTES, DOODLES, ETC:

○

TITLE: _____

AUTHOR: _____

ILLUSTRATOR: _____

DATE FINISHED: _____ #PAGES: ___

STORY SHARED BY: _____

_____

DID WE LIKE IT? ☆ ☆ ☆ ☆ ☆

NOTES, DOODLES, ETC:

○

TITLE: _____

AUTHOR: _____

ILLUSTRATOR: _____

DATE FINISHED: _____ # PAGES: ___

STORY SHARED BY: _____

DID WE LIKE IT? ☆ ☆ ☆ ☆ ☆

NOTES, DOODLES, ETC:

○

TITLE: _____

AUTHOR: _____

ILLUSTRATOR: _____

DATE FINISHED: _____ # PAGES: ___

STORY SHARED BY: _____

DID WE LIKE IT? ☆ ☆ ☆ ☆ ☆

NOTES, DOODLES, ETC:

○

TITLE: _____

AUTHOR: _____

ILLUSTRATOR: _____

DATE FINISHED: _____ # PAGES: ___

STORY SHARED BY: _____

DID WE LIKE IT? ☆ ☆ ☆ ☆ ☆

NOTES, DOODLES, ETC:

○

TITLE: _____

AUTHOR: _____

ILLUSTRATOR: _____

DATE FINISHED: _____ # PAGES: ___

STORY SHARED BY: _____

DID WE LIKE IT? ☆ ☆ ☆ ☆ ☆

NOTES, DOODLES, ETC:

○

TITLE: _____
AUTHOR: _____
ILLUSTRATOR: _____
DATE FINISHED: _____ #PAGES: ___
STORY SHARED BY: _____
_____

DID WE LIKE IT?   ☆ ☆ ☆ ☆ ☆
NOTES, DOODLES, ETC:

○

TITLE: _____
AUTHOR: _____
ILLUSTRATOR: _____
DATE FINISHED: _____ #PAGES: ___
STORY SHARED BY: _____
_____

DID WE LIKE IT?   ☆ ☆ ☆ ☆ ☆
NOTES, DOODLES, ETC:

○

TITLE: _____
AUTHOR: _____
ILLUSTRATOR: _____
DATE FINISHED: _____ #PAGES: ___
STORY SHARED BY: _____
_____

DID WE LIKE IT?   ☆ ☆ ☆ ☆ ☆
NOTES, DOODLES, ETC:

○

TITLE: _____
AUTHOR: _____
ILLUSTRATOR: _____
DATE FINISHED: _____ #PAGES: ___
STORY SHARED BY: _____

Did we like it? ☆ ☆ ☆ ☆ ☆
NOTES, DOODLES, ETC:

TITLE: _____
AUTHOR: _____
ILLUSTRATOR: _____
DATE FINISHED: _____ #PAGES: ___
STORY SHARED BY: _____

Did we like it? ☆ ☆ ☆ ☆ ☆
NOTES, DOODLES, ETC:

TITLE: _____
AUTHOR: _____
ILLUSTRATOR: _____
DATE FINISHED: _____ #PAGES: ___
STORY SHARED BY: _____

Did we like it? ☆ ☆ ☆ ☆ ☆
NOTES, DOODLES, ETC:

"A room
    without books
  is like a body
    without a soul."

— Marcus Tullius Cicero

TITLE: _____

AUTHOR: _____

ILLUSTRATOR: _____

DATE FINISHED: _____ #PAGES: ___

STORY SHARED BY: _____

DID WE LIKE IT? ☆ ☆ ☆ ☆ ☆

NOTES, DOODLES, ETC:

TITLE: _____

AUTHOR: _____

ILLUSTRATOR: _____

DATE FINISHED: _____ #PAGES: ___

STORY SHARED BY: _____

DID WE LIKE IT? ☆ ☆ ☆ ☆ ☆

NOTES, DOODLES, ETC:

TITLE: _____

AUTHOR: _____

ILLUSTRATOR: _____

DATE FINISHED: _____ #PAGES: ___

STORY SHARED BY: _____

DID WE LIKE IT? ☆ ☆ ☆ ☆ ☆

NOTES, DOODLES, ETC:

TITLE: _____

AUTHOR: _____

ILLUSTRATOR: _____

DATE FINISHED: _____ #PAGES: ___

STORY SHARED BY: _____

DID WE LIKE IT? ☆ ☆ ☆ ☆ ☆

NOTES, DOODLES, ETC:

TITLE: _____
AUTHOR: _____
ILLUSTRATOR: _____
DATE FINISHED: _____ #PAGES: ___
STORY SHARED BY: _____

DID WE LIKE IT? ☆ ☆ ☆ ☆ ☆
NOTES, DOODLES, ETC:

TITLE: _____
AUTHOR: _____
ILLUSTRATOR: _____
DATE FINISHED: _____ #PAGES: ___
STORY SHARED BY: _____

DID WE LIKE IT? ☆ ☆ ☆ ☆ ☆
NOTES, DOODLES, ETC:

TITLE: _____
AUTHOR: _____
ILLUSTRATOR: _____
DATE FINISHED: _____ #PAGES: ___
STORY SHARED BY: _____

DID WE LIKE IT? ☆ ☆ ☆ ☆ ☆
NOTES, DOODLES, ETC:

TITLE: _____
AUTHOR: _____
ILLUSTRATOR: _____
DATE FINISHED: _____ #PAGES: ___
STORY SHARED BY: _____

DID WE LIKE IT? ☆ ☆ ☆ ☆ ☆
NOTES, DOODLES, ETC:

TITLE: _____

AUTHOR: _____

ILLUSTRATOR: _____

DATE FINISHED: _____ # PAGES: ____

STORY SHARED BY: _____

Did we like it? ☆ ☆ ☆ ☆ ☆

NOTES, DOODLES, ETC:

TITLE: _____

AUTHOR: _____

ILLUSTRATOR: _____

DATE FINISHED: _____ # PAGES: ____

STORY SHARED BY: _____

Did we like it? ☆ ☆ ☆ ☆ ☆

NOTES, DOODLES, ETC:

TITLE: _____

AUTHOR: _____

ILLUSTRATOR: _____

DATE FINISHED: _____ # PAGES: ____

STORY SHARED BY: _____

Did we like it? ☆ ☆ ☆ ☆ ☆

NOTES, DOODLES, ETC:

TITLE: _____

AUTHOR: _____

ILLUSTRATOR: _____

DATE FINISHED: _____ # PAGES: ____

STORY SHARED BY: _____

Did we like it? ☆ ☆ ☆ ☆ ☆

NOTES, DOODLES, ETC:

TITLE: _____

AUTHOR: _____

ILLUSTRATOR: _____

DATE FINISHED: _____ # PAGES: ___

STORY SHARED BY: _____

Did WE LIKE iT? ☆ ☆ ☆ ☆ ☆

NOTES, DOODLES, ETC:

"What refuge is there
for the victim
who is oppressed
with the feeling
that there are
a thousand new books
he ought to read,
while life is only
long enough for him
to attempt to read
a hundred?"

— Oliver Wendell Holmes Sr., **Over the Teacups**

TITLE: _____

AUTHOR: _____

ILLUSTRATOR: _____

DATE FINISHED: _____ # PAGES: ___

STORY SHARED BY: _____

DID WE LIKE iT? ☆ ☆ ☆ ☆ ☆

NOTES, DOODLES, ETC:

TITLE: _____

AUTHOR: _____

ILLUSTRATOR: _____

DATE FINISHED: _____ # PAGES: ___

STORY SHARED BY: _____

DID WE LIKE iT? ☆ ☆ ☆ ☆ ☆

NOTES, DOODLES, ETC:

TITLE: _____

AUTHOR: _____

ILLUSTRATOR: _____

DATE FINISHED: _____   #PAGES: ___

STORY SHARED BY: _____

_____

DID WE LIKE IT?   ☆ ☆ ☆ ☆ ☆

NOTES, DOODLES, ETC:

○

TITLE: _____

AUTHOR: _____

ILLUSTRATOR: _____

DATE FINISHED: _____   #PAGES: ___

STORY SHARED BY: _____

_____

DID WE LIKE IT?   ☆ ☆ ☆ ☆ ☆

NOTES, DOODLES, ETC:

○

TITLE: _____

AUTHOR: _____

ILLUSTRATOR: _____

DATE FINISHED: _____   #PAGES: ___

STORY SHARED BY: _____

_____

DID WE LIKE IT?   ☆ ☆ ☆ ☆ ☆

NOTES, DOODLES, ETC:

○

TITLE: _____

AUTHOR: _____

ILLUSTRATOR: _____

DATE FINISHED: _____   #PAGES: ___

STORY SHARED BY: _____

_____

DID WE LIKE IT?   ☆ ☆ ☆ ☆ ☆

NOTES, DOODLES, ETC:

○

TITLE: _____
AUTHOR: _____
ILLUSTRATOR: _____
DATE FINISHED: _____ #PAGES: __
STORY SHARED BY: _____

DID WE LIKE IT? ☆☆☆☆☆
NOTES, DOODLES, ETC:

TITLE: _____
AUTHOR: _____
ILLUSTRATOR: _____
DATE FINISHED: _____ #PAGES: __
STORY SHARED BY: _____

DID WE LIKE IT? ☆☆☆☆☆
NOTES, DOODLES, ETC:

TITLE: _____
AUTHOR: _____
ILLUSTRATOR: _____
DATE FINISHED: _____ #PAGES: __
STORY SHARED BY: _____

DID WE LIKE IT? ☆☆☆☆☆
NOTES, DOODLES, ETC:

TITLE: _____
AUTHOR: _____
ILLUSTRATOR: _____
DATE FINISHED: _____ #PAGES: __
STORY SHARED BY: _____

DID WE LIKE IT? ☆☆☆☆☆
NOTES, DOODLES, ETC:

TITLE: _____

AUTHOR: _____

ILLUSTRATOR: _____

DATE FINISHED: _____ #PAGES: ___

STORY SHARED BY: _____

_____

DID WE LIKE IT?   ☆ ☆ ☆ ☆ ☆

NOTES, DOODLES, ETC:

○

TITLE: _____

AUTHOR: _____

ILLUSTRATOR: _____

DATE FINISHED: _____ #PAGES: ___

STORY SHARED BY: _____

_____

DID WE LIKE IT?   ☆ ☆ ☆ ☆ ☆

NOTES, DOODLES, ETC:

○

TITLE: _____

AUTHOR: _____

ILLUSTRATOR: _____

DATE FINISHED: _____ #PAGES: ___

STORY SHARED BY: _____

_____

DID WE LIKE IT?   ☆ ☆ ☆ ☆ ☆

NOTES, DOODLES, ETC:

○

TITLE: _____

AUTHOR: _____

ILLUSTRATOR: _____

DATE FINISHED: _____ #PAGES: ___

STORY SHARED BY: _____

_____

DID WE LIKE IT?   ☆ ☆ ☆ ☆ ☆

NOTES, DOODLES, ETC:

○

TITLE: _____
AUTHOR: _____
ILLUSTRATOR: _____
DATE FINISHED: _____ #PAGES: ___
STORY SHARED BY: _____

_____

DID WE LIKE IT? ☆ ☆ ☆ ☆ ☆
NOTES, DOODLES, ETC:

○

TITLE: _____
AUTHOR: _____
ILLUSTRATOR: _____
DATE FINISHED: _____ #PAGES: ___
STORY SHARED BY: _____

_____

DID WE LIKE IT? ☆ ☆ ☆ ☆ ☆
NOTES, DOODLES, ETC:

○

TITLE: _____
AUTHOR: _____
ILLUSTRATOR: _____
DATE FINISHED: _____ #PAGES: ___
STORY SHARED BY: _____

_____

DID WE LIKE IT? ☆ ☆ ☆ ☆ ☆
NOTES, DOODLES, ETC:

○

TITLE: _____

AUTHOR: _____

ILLUSTRATOR: _____

DATE FINISHED: _____ #PAGES: ___

STORY SHARED BY: _____

_____

DID WE LIKE IT? ☆ ☆ ☆ ☆ ☆

NOTES, DOODLES, ETC:

○

TITLE: _____

AUTHOR: _____

ILLUSTRATOR: _____

DATE FINISHED: _____ #PAGES: ___

STORY SHARED BY: _____

_____

DID WE LIKE IT? ☆ ☆ ☆ ☆ ☆

NOTES, DOODLES, ETC:

○

TITLE: _____

AUTHOR: _____

ILLUSTRATOR: _____

DATE FINISHED: _____ #PAGES: ___

STORY SHARED BY: _____

_____

DID WE LIKE IT? ☆ ☆ ☆ ☆ ☆

NOTES, DOODLES, ETC:

○

TITLE: _____

AUTHOR: _____

ILLUSTRATOR: _____

DATE FINISHED: _____ #PAGES: ___

STORY SHARED BY: _____

_____

DID WE LIKE IT? ☆ ☆ ☆ ☆ ☆

NOTES, DOODLES, ETC:

○

TITLE: _____

AUTHOR: _____

ILLUSTRATOR: _____

DATE FINISHED: _____ #PAGES: _____

STORY SHARED BY: _____

DID WE LIKE IT? ☆ ☆ ☆ ☆ ☆

NOTES, DOODLES, ETC:

○

TITLE: _____

AUTHOR: _____

ILLUSTRATOR: _____

DATE FINISHED: _____ #PAGES: _____

STORY SHARED BY: _____

DID WE LIKE IT? ☆ ☆ ☆ ☆ ☆

NOTES, DOODLES, ETC:

○

TITLE: _____

AUTHOR: _____

ILLUSTRATOR: _____

DATE FINISHED: _____ #PAGES: _____

STORY SHARED BY: _____

DID WE LIKE IT? ☆ ☆ ☆ ☆ ☆

NOTES, DOODLES, ETC:

○

TITLE: _____

AUTHOR: _____

ILLUSTRATOR: _____

DATE FINISHED: _____ #PAGES: _____

STORY SHARED BY: _____

DID WE LIKE IT? ☆ ☆ ☆ ☆ ☆

NOTES, DOODLES, ETC:

○

TITLE: _____
AUTHOR: _____
ILLUSTRATOR: _____
DATE FINISHED: _____ # PAGES: _____
STORY SHARED BY: _____
_____
Did we like it? ☆ ☆ ☆ ☆ ☆
NOTES, DOODLES, ETC:

TITLE: _____
AUTHOR: _____
ILLUSTRATOR: _____
DATE FINISHED: _____ # PAGES: _____
STORY SHARED BY: _____
_____
Did we like it? ☆ ☆ ☆ ☆ ☆
NOTES, DOODLES, ETC:

"What we become
    depends on what
    we read after
       all of the professors
    have finished with us.
    The greatest
       university of all
    is a collection
       of books."

— Thomas Carlyle

TITLE: _____
AUTHOR: _____
ILLUSTRATOR: _____
DATE FINISHED: _____ # PAGES: _____
STORY SHARED BY: _____
_____
Did we like it? ☆ ☆ ☆ ☆ ☆
NOTES, DOODLES, ETC:

TITLE: _____

AUTHOR: _____

ILLUSTRATOR: _____

DATE FINISHED: _____ # PAGES: ____

STORY SHARED BY: _____

Did we like it? ☆ ☆ ☆ ☆ ☆

NOTES, DOODLES, ETC:

TITLE: _____

AUTHOR: _____

ILLUSTRATOR: _____

DATE FINISHED: _____ # PAGES: ____

STORY SHARED BY: _____

Did we like it? ☆ ☆ ☆ ☆ ☆

NOTES, DOODLES, ETC:

TITLE: _____

AUTHOR: _____

ILLUSTRATOR: _____

DATE FINISHED: _____ # PAGES: ____

STORY SHARED BY: _____

Did we like it? ☆ ☆ ☆ ☆ ☆

NOTES, DOODLES, ETC:

TITLE: _____

AUTHOR: _____

ILLUSTRATOR: _____

DATE FINISHED: _____ # PAGES: ____

STORY SHARED BY: _____

Did we like it? ☆ ☆ ☆ ☆ ☆

NOTES, DOODLES, ETC:

TITLE: _____
AUTHOR: _____
ILLUSTRATOR: _____
DATE FINISHED: _____ #PAGES: ___
STORY SHARED BY: _____
_____
DID WE LIKE IT? ☆ ☆ ☆ ☆ ☆
NOTES, DOODLES, ETC:

○

TITLE: _____
AUTHOR: _____
ILLUSTRATOR: _____
DATE FINISHED: _____ #PAGES: ___
STORY SHARED BY: _____
_____
DID WE LIKE IT? ☆ ☆ ☆ ☆ ☆
NOTES, DOODLES, ETC:

○

TITLE: _____
AUTHOR: _____
ILLUSTRATOR: _____
DATE FINISHED: _____ #PAGES: ___
STORY SHARED BY: _____
_____
DID WE LIKE IT? ☆ ☆ ☆ ☆ ☆
NOTES, DOODLES, ETC:

○

TITLE: _____
AUTHOR: _____
ILLUSTRATOR: _____
DATE FINISHED: _____ #PAGES: ___
STORY SHARED BY: _____
_____
DID WE LIKE IT? ☆ ☆ ☆ ☆ ☆
NOTES, DOODLES, ETC:

○

TITLE: _____
AUTHOR: _____
ILLUSTRATOR: _____
DATE FINISHED: _____ #PAGES: _____
STORY SHARED BY: _____

DID WE LIKE IT? ☆ ☆ ☆ ☆ ☆
NOTES, DOODLES, ETC:

"Wear the
      old coat
and buy
      the new book."

— Austin Phelps

TITLE: _____
AUTHOR: _____
ILLUSTRATOR: _____
DATE FINISHED: _____ #PAGES: _____
STORY SHARED BY: _____

DID WE LIKE IT? ☆ ☆ ☆ ☆ ☆
NOTES, DOODLES, ETC:

TITLE: _____
AUTHOR: _____
ILLUSTRATOR: _____
DATE FINISHED: _____ #PAGES: _____
STORY SHARED BY: _____

DID WE LIKE IT? ☆ ☆ ☆ ☆ ☆
NOTES, DOODLES, ETC:

TITLE: _____
AUTHOR: _____
ILLUSTRATOR: _____
DATE FINISHED: _____ # PAGES: ___
STORY SHARED BY: _____
_____
DID WE LIKE IT? ☆ ☆ ☆ ☆ ☆
NOTES, DOODLES, ETC:

TITLE: _____
AUTHOR: _____
ILLUSTRATOR: _____
DATE FINISHED: _____ # PAGES: ___
STORY SHARED BY: _____
_____
DID WE LIKE IT? ☆ ☆ ☆ ☆ ☆
NOTES, DOODLES, ETC:

TITLE: _____
AUTHOR: _____
ILLUSTRATOR: _____
DATE FINISHED: _____ # PAGES: ___
STORY SHARED BY: _____
_____
DID WE LIKE IT? ☆ ☆ ☆ ☆ ☆
NOTES, DOODLES, ETC:

TITLE: _____
AUTHOR: _____
ILLUSTRATOR: _____
DATE FINISHED: _____ # PAGES: ___
STORY SHARED BY: _____
_____
DID WE LIKE IT? ☆ ☆ ☆ ☆ ☆
NOTES, DOODLES, ETC:

TITLE: _____

AUTHOR: _____

ILLUSTRATOR: _____

DATE FINISHED: _____ # PAGES: ___

STORY SHARED BY: _____

Did we like it? ☆ ☆ ☆ ☆ ☆

NOTES, DOODLES, ETC:

○

TITLE: _____

AUTHOR: _____

ILLUSTRATOR: _____

DATE FINISHED: _____ # PAGES: ___

STORY SHARED BY: _____

Did we like it? ☆ ☆ ☆ ☆ ☆

NOTES, DOODLES, ETC:

○

TITLE: _____

AUTHOR: _____

ILLUSTRATOR: _____

DATE FINISHED: _____ # PAGES: ___

STORY SHARED BY: _____

Did we like it? ☆ ☆ ☆ ☆ ☆

NOTES, DOODLES, ETC:

○

TITLE: _____

AUTHOR: _____

ILLUSTRATOR: _____

DATE FINISHED: _____ # PAGES: ___

STORY SHARED BY: _____

Did we like it? ☆ ☆ ☆ ☆ ☆

NOTES, DOODLES, ETC:

○

TITLE: _____
AUTHOR: _____
ILLUSTRATOR: _____
DATE FINISHED: _____ # PAGES: ___
STORY SHARED BY: _____

Did we like it?   ☆ ☆ ☆ ☆ ☆
NOTES, DOODLES, ETC:

○

TITLE: _____
AUTHOR: _____
ILLUSTRATOR: _____
DATE FINISHED: _____ # PAGES: ___
STORY SHARED BY: _____

Did we like it?   ☆ ☆ ☆ ☆ ☆
NOTES, DOODLES, ETC:

○

TITLE: _____
AUTHOR: _____
ILLUSTRATOR: _____
DATE FINISHED: _____ # PAGES: ___
STORY SHARED BY: _____

Did we like it?   ☆ ☆ ☆ ☆ ☆
NOTES, DOODLES, ETC:

○

TITLE: _____
AUTHOR: _____
ILLUSTRATOR: _____
DATE FINISHED: _____ # PAGES: ___
STORY SHARED BY: _____

Did we like it?   ☆ ☆ ☆ ☆ ☆
NOTES, DOODLES, ETC:

○

TITLE: _____
AUTHOR: _____
ILLUSTRATOR: _____
DATE FINISHED: _____ #PAGES: ___
STORY SHARED BY: _____

DID WE LIKE IT? ☆ ☆ ☆ ☆ ☆
NOTES, DOODLES, ETC:

○

TITLE: _____
AUTHOR: _____
ILLUSTRATOR: _____
DATE FINISHED: _____ #PAGES: ___
STORY SHARED BY: _____

DID WE LIKE IT? ☆ ☆ ☆ ☆ ☆
NOTES, DOODLES, ETC:

○

TITLE: _____
AUTHOR: _____
ILLUSTRATOR: _____
DATE FINISHED: _____ #PAGES: ___
STORY SHARED BY: _____

DID WE LIKE IT? ☆ ☆ ☆ ☆ ☆
NOTES, DOODLES, ETC:

○

TITLE: _____

AUTHOR: _____

ILLUSTRATOR: _____

DATE FINISHED: _____ #PAGES: ____

STORY SHARED BY: _____

_____

DID WE LIKE IT?   ☆ ☆ ☆ ☆ ☆

NOTES, DOODLES, ETC:

○

TITLE: _____

AUTHOR: _____

ILLUSTRATOR: _____

DATE FINISHED: _____ #PAGES: ____

STORY SHARED BY: _____

_____

DID WE LIKE IT?   ☆ ☆ ☆ ☆ ☆

NOTES, DOODLES, ETC:

○

TITLE: _____

AUTHOR: _____

ILLUSTRATOR: _____

DATE FINISHED: _____ #PAGES: ____

STORY SHARED BY: _____

_____

DID WE LIKE IT?   ☆ ☆ ☆ ☆ ☆

NOTES, DOODLES, ETC:

○

TITLE: _____

AUTHOR: _____

ILLUSTRATOR: _____

DATE FINISHED: _____ #PAGES: ____

STORY SHARED BY: _____

_____

DID WE LIKE IT?   ☆ ☆ ☆ ☆ ☆

NOTES, DOODLES, ETC:

○

TITLE: _____

AUTHOR: _____

ILLUSTRATOR: _____

DATE FINISHED: _____ # PAGES: ___

STORY SHARED BY: _____

DID WE LIKE IT? ☆ ☆ ☆ ☆ ☆

NOTES, DOODLES, ETC:

○

TITLE: _____

AUTHOR: _____

ILLUSTRATOR: _____

DATE FINISHED: _____ # PAGES: ___

STORY SHARED BY: _____

DID WE LIKE IT? ☆ ☆ ☆ ☆ ☆

NOTES, DOODLES, ETC:

○

TITLE: _____

AUTHOR: _____

ILLUSTRATOR: _____

DATE FINISHED: _____ # PAGES: ___

STORY SHARED BY: _____

DID WE LIKE IT? ☆ ☆ ☆ ☆ ☆

NOTES, DOODLES, ETC:

○

TITLE: _____

AUTHOR: _____

ILLUSTRATOR: _____

DATE FINISHED: _____ # PAGES: ___

STORY SHARED BY: _____

DID WE LIKE IT? ☆ ☆ ☆ ☆ ☆

NOTES, DOODLES, ETC:

○

TITLE: _____
AUTHOR: _____
ILLUSTRATOR: _____
DATE FINISHED: _____ #PAGES: ___
STORY SHARED BY: _____

Did we like it? ☆ ☆ ☆ ☆ ☆
NOTES, DOODLES, ETC:

◯

TITLE: _____
AUTHOR: _____
ILLUSTRATOR: _____
DATE FINISHED: _____ #PAGES: ___
STORY SHARED BY: _____

Did we like it? ☆ ☆ ☆ ☆ ☆
NOTES, DOODLES, ETC:

◯

TITLE: _____
AUTHOR: _____
ILLUSTRATOR: _____
DATE FINISHED: _____ #PAGES: ___
STORY SHARED BY: _____

Did we like it? ☆ ☆ ☆ ☆ ☆
NOTES, DOODLES, ETC:

◯

TITLE: _____
AUTHOR: _____
ILLUSTRATOR: _____
DATE FINISHED: _____ #PAGES: ___
STORY SHARED BY: _____

Did we like it? ☆ ☆ ☆ ☆ ☆
NOTES, DOODLES, ETC:

◯

TITLE: _____
AUTHOR: _____
ILLUSTRATOR: _____
DATE FINISHED: _____ #PAGES: ___
STORY SHARED BY: _____

DID WE LIKE IT? ☆ ☆ ☆ ☆ ☆
NOTES, DOODLES, ETC:

○

TITLE: _____
AUTHOR: _____
ILLUSTRATOR: _____
DATE FINISHED: _____ #PAGES: ___
STORY SHARED BY: _____

DID WE LIKE IT? ☆ ☆ ☆ ☆ ☆
NOTES, DOODLES, ETC:

○

TITLE: _____
AUTHOR: _____
ILLUSTRATOR: _____
DATE FINISHED: _____ #PAGES: ___
STORY SHARED BY: _____

DID WE LIKE IT? ☆ ☆ ☆ ☆ ☆
NOTES, DOODLES, ETC:

○

TITLE: _____
AUTHOR: _____
ILLUSTRATOR: _____
DATE FINISHED: _____ #PAGES: ___
STORY SHARED BY: _____

DID WE LIKE IT? ☆ ☆ ☆ ☆ ☆
NOTES, DOODLES, ETC:

○

> "Some books are
> so familiar
> that reading them
> is like
> being home
> again."

— Louisa May Alcott, **Little Women**

TITLE: _____

AUTHOR: _____

ILLUSTRATOR: _____

DATE FINISHED: _____ #PAGES: ____

STORY SHARED BY: _____

_____

DID WE LIKE IT? ☆ ☆ ☆ ☆ ☆

NOTES, DOODLES, ETC:

TITLE: _____

AUTHOR: _____

ILLUSTRATOR: _____

DATE FINISHED: _____ #PAGES: ____

STORY SHARED BY: _____

_____

DID WE LIKE IT? ☆ ☆ ☆ ☆ ☆

NOTES, DOODLES, ETC:

TITLE: _____

AUTHOR: _____

ILLUSTRATOR: _____

DATE FINISHED: _____ #PAGES: ____

STORY SHARED BY: _____

_____

DID WE LIKE IT? ☆ ☆ ☆ ☆ ☆

NOTES, DOODLES, ETC:

TITLE: _____

AUTHOR: _____

ILLUSTRATOR: _____

DATE FINISHED: _____ # PAGES: ___

STORY SHARED BY: _____

Did we like it? ☆ ☆ ☆ ☆ ☆

NOTES, DOODLES, ETC:

○

TITLE: _____

AUTHOR: _____

ILLUSTRATOR: _____

DATE FINISHED: _____ # PAGES: ___

STORY SHARED BY: _____

Did we like it? ☆ ☆ ☆ ☆ ☆

NOTES, DOODLES, ETC:

○

TITLE: _____

AUTHOR: _____

ILLUSTRATOR: _____

DATE FINISHED: _____ # PAGES: ___

STORY SHARED BY: _____

Did we like it? ☆ ☆ ☆ ☆ ☆

NOTES, DOODLES, ETC:

○

TITLE: _____

AUTHOR: _____

ILLUSTRATOR: _____

DATE FINISHED: _____ # PAGES: ___

STORY SHARED BY: _____

Did we like it? ☆ ☆ ☆ ☆ ☆

NOTES, DOODLES, ETC:

○

TITLE: _____
AUTHOR: _____
ILLUSTRATOR: _____
DATE FINISHED: _____ #PAGES: ____
STORY SHARED BY: _____

Did we like it? ☆ ☆ ☆ ☆ ☆
NOTES, DOODLES, ETC:

TITLE: _____
AUTHOR: _____
ILLUSTRATOR: _____
DATE FINISHED: _____ #PAGES: ____
STORY SHARED BY: _____

Did we like it? ☆ ☆ ☆ ☆ ☆
NOTES, DOODLES, ETC:

TITLE: _____
AUTHOR: _____
ILLUSTRATOR: _____
DATE FINISHED: _____ #PAGES: ____
STORY SHARED BY: _____

Did we like it? ☆ ☆ ☆ ☆ ☆
NOTES, DOODLES, ETC:

TITLE: _____
AUTHOR: _____
ILLUSTRATOR: _____
DATE FINISHED: _____ #PAGES: ____
STORY SHARED BY: _____

Did we like it? ☆ ☆ ☆ ☆ ☆
NOTES, DOODLES, ETC:

TITLE: _____
AUTHOR: _____
ILLUSTRATOR: _____
DATE FINISHED: _____ # PAGES: ___
STORY SHARED BY: _____

Did we like it?   ☆ ☆ ☆ ☆ ☆
Notes, doodles, etc:

"There are
chance meetings
with strangers
that interest us from
the first moment,
before a word
is spoken."

— Fyodor Dostoyevsky, **Crime and Punishment**

TITLE: _____
AUTHOR: _____
ILLUSTRATOR: _____
DATE FINISHED: _____ # PAGES: ___
STORY SHARED BY: _____

Did we like it?   ☆ ☆ ☆ ☆ ☆
Notes, doodles, etc:

TITLE: _____
AUTHOR: _____
ILLUSTRATOR: _____
DATE FINISHED: _____ #PAGES: ___
STORY SHARED BY: _____

Did we like it?   ☆ ☆ ☆ ☆ ☆
Notes, doodles, etc:

TITLE: _____
AUTHOR: _____
ILLUSTRATOR: _____
DATE FINISHED: _____ #PAGES: ___
STORY SHARED BY: _____

_____
DID WE LIKE IT? ☆ ☆ ☆ ☆ ☆
NOTES, DOODLES, ETC:

TITLE: _____
AUTHOR: _____
ILLUSTRATOR: _____
DATE FINISHED: _____ #PAGES: ___
STORY SHARED BY: _____

_____
DID WE LIKE IT? ☆ ☆ ☆ ☆ ☆
NOTES, DOODLES, ETC:

TITLE: _____
AUTHOR: _____
ILLUSTRATOR: _____
DATE FINISHED: _____ #PAGES: ___
STORY SHARED BY: _____

_____
DID WE LIKE IT? ☆ ☆ ☆ ☆ ☆
NOTES, DOODLES, ETC:

TITLE: _____
AUTHOR: _____
ILLUSTRATOR: _____
DATE FINISHED: _____ #PAGES: ___
STORY SHARED BY: _____

_____
DID WE LIKE IT? ☆ ☆ ☆ ☆ ☆
NOTES, DOODLES, ETC:

TITLE: _____
AUTHOR: _____
ILLUSTRATOR: _____
DATE FINISHED: _____ #PAGES: ___
STORY SHARED BY: _____

Did we like it? ☆ ☆ ☆ ☆ ☆
NOTES, DOODLES, ETC:

TITLE: _____
AUTHOR: _____
ILLUSTRATOR: _____
DATE FINISHED: _____ #PAGES: ___
STORY SHARED BY: _____

Did we like it? ☆ ☆ ☆ ☆ ☆
NOTES, DOODLES, ETC:

TITLE: _____
AUTHOR: _____
ILLUSTRATOR: _____
DATE FINISHED: _____ #PAGES: ___
STORY SHARED BY: _____

Did we like it? ☆ ☆ ☆ ☆ ☆
NOTES, DOODLES, ETC:

TITLE: _____
AUTHOR: _____
ILLUSTRATOR: _____
DATE FINISHED: _____ #PAGES: ___
STORY SHARED BY: _____

Did we like it? ☆ ☆ ☆ ☆ ☆
NOTES, DOODLES, ETC:

TITLE: _____
AUTHOR: _____
ILLUSTRATOR: _____
DATE FINISHED: _____ #PAGES: ___
STORY SHARED BY: _____

DID WE LIKE IT? ☆ ☆ ☆ ☆ ☆
NOTES, DOODLES, ETC:

○

TITLE: _____
AUTHOR: _____
ILLUSTRATOR: _____
DATE FINISHED: _____ #PAGES: ___
STORY SHARED BY: _____

DID WE LIKE IT? ☆ ☆ ☆ ☆ ☆
NOTES, DOODLES, ETC:

○

"Fairy tales say that
apples were golden
only to refresh
the forgotten moment
when we found that
they were green.
They make rivers run
with wine
only to make us
remember, for one
wild moment,
that they run
with water."

— G. K. Chesterton, **Orthodoxy**

TITLE: _____
AUTHOR: _____
ILLUSTRATOR: _____
DATE FINISHED: _____ #PAGES: ___
STORY SHARED BY: _____

DID WE LIKE IT? ☆ ☆ ☆ ☆ ☆
NOTES, DOODLES, ETC:

○

TITLE: _____
AUTHOR: _____
ILLUSTRATOR: _____
DATE FINISHED: _____ #PAGES: ___
STORY SHARED BY: _____
_____

DID WE LIKE IT? ☆ ☆ ☆ ☆ ☆
NOTES, DOODLES, ETC:

○

TITLE: _____
AUTHOR: _____
ILLUSTRATOR: _____
DATE FINISHED: _____ #PAGES: ___
STORY SHARED BY: _____
_____

DID WE LIKE IT? ☆ ☆ ☆ ☆ ☆
NOTES, DOODLES, ETC:

○

TITLE: _____
AUTHOR: _____
ILLUSTRATOR: _____
DATE FINISHED: _____ #PAGES: ___
STORY SHARED BY: _____
_____

DID WE LIKE IT? ☆ ☆ ☆ ☆ ☆
NOTES, DOODLES, ETC:

○

TITLE: _____
AUTHOR: _____
ILLUSTRATOR: _____
DATE FINISHED: _____ #PAGES: ___
STORY SHARED BY: _____
_____

DID WE LIKE IT? ☆ ☆ ☆ ☆ ☆
NOTES, DOODLES, ETC:

○

TITLE: _____

AUTHOR: _____

ILLUSTRATOR: _____

DATE FINISHED: _____ # PAGES: ___

STORY SHARED BY: _____

Did we like it? ☆ ☆ ☆ ☆ ☆

NOTES, DOODLES, ETC:

TITLE: _____

AUTHOR: _____

ILLUSTRATOR: _____

DATE FINISHED: _____ # PAGES: ___

STORY SHARED BY: _____

Did we like it? ☆ ☆ ☆ ☆ ☆

NOTES, DOODLES, ETC:

TITLE: _____

AUTHOR: _____

ILLUSTRATOR: _____

DATE FINISHED: _____ # PAGES: ___

STORY SHARED BY: _____

Did we like it? ☆ ☆ ☆ ☆ ☆

NOTES, DOODLES, ETC:

TITLE: _____

AUTHOR: _____

ILLUSTRATOR: _____

DATE FINISHED: _____ # PAGES: ___

STORY SHARED BY: _____

Did we like it? ☆ ☆ ☆ ☆ ☆

NOTES, DOODLES, ETC:

TITLE: _____

AUTHOR: _____

ILLUSTRATOR: _____

DATE FINISHED: _____ #PAGES: __

STORY SHARED BY: _____

_____

DID WE LIKE IT?   ☆ ☆ ☆ ☆ ☆

NOTES, DOODLES, ETC:

○

TITLE: _____

AUTHOR: _____

ILLUSTRATOR: _____

DATE FINISHED: _____ #PAGES: __

STORY SHARED BY: _____

_____

DID WE LIKE IT?   ☆ ☆ ☆ ☆ ☆

NOTES, DOODLES, ETC:

○

TITLE: _____

AUTHOR: _____

ILLUSTRATOR: _____

DATE FINISHED: _____ #PAGES: __

STORY SHARED BY: _____

_____

DID WE LIKE IT?   ☆ ☆ ☆ ☆ ☆

NOTES, DOODLES, ETC:

○

TITLE: _____

AUTHOR: _____

ILLUSTRATOR: _____

DATE FINISHED: _____ #PAGES: __

STORY SHARED BY: _____

_____

DID WE LIKE IT?   ☆ ☆ ☆ ☆ ☆

NOTES, DOODLES, ETC:

○

TITLE: _____

AUTHOR: _____

ILLUSTRATOR: _____

DATE FINISHED: _____ # PAGES: ___

STORY SHARED BY: _____

Did we like it? ☆ ☆ ☆ ☆ ☆

Notes, Doodles, etc:

TITLE: _____

AUTHOR: _____

ILLUSTRATOR: _____

DATE FINISHED: _____ # PAGES: ___

STORY SHARED BY: _____

Did we like it? ☆ ☆ ☆ ☆ ☆

Notes, Doodles, etc:

TITLE: _____

AUTHOR: _____

ILLUSTRATOR: _____

DATE FINISHED: _____ # PAGES: ___

STORY SHARED BY: _____

Did we like it? ☆ ☆ ☆ ☆ ☆

Notes, Doodles, etc:

TITLE: _____
AUTHOR: _____
ILLUSTRATOR: _____
DATE FINISHED: _____ #PAGES: ___
STORY SHARED BY: _____

DID WE LIKE IT? ☆ ☆ ☆ ☆ ☆
NOTES, DOODLES, ETC:

TITLE: _____
AUTHOR: _____
ILLUSTRATOR: _____
DATE FINISHED: _____ #PAGES: ___
STORY SHARED BY: _____

DID WE LIKE IT? ☆ ☆ ☆ ☆ ☆
NOTES, DOODLES, ETC:

TITLE: _____
AUTHOR: _____
ILLUSTRATOR: _____
DATE FINISHED: _____ #PAGES: ___
STORY SHARED BY: _____

DID WE LIKE IT? ☆ ☆ ☆ ☆ ☆
NOTES, DOODLES, ETC:

TITLE: _____
AUTHOR: _____
ILLUSTRATOR: _____
DATE FINISHED: _____ #PAGES: ___
STORY SHARED BY: _____

DID WE LIKE IT? ☆ ☆ ☆ ☆ ☆
NOTES, DOODLES, ETC:

TITLE: _____
AUTHOR: _____
ILLUSTRATOR: _____
DATE FINISHED: _____ #PAGES: ____
STORY SHARED BY: _____

Did we like it? ☆ ☆ ☆ ☆ ☆
NOTES, DOODLES, ETC:

○

TITLE: _____
AUTHOR: _____
ILLUSTRATOR: _____
DATE FINISHED: _____ #PAGES: ____
STORY SHARED BY: _____

Did we like it? ☆ ☆ ☆ ☆ ☆
NOTES, DOODLES, ETC:

○

TITLE: _____
AUTHOR: _____
ILLUSTRATOR: _____
DATE FINISHED: _____ #PAGES: ____
STORY SHARED BY: _____

Did we like it? ☆ ☆ ☆ ☆ ☆
NOTES, DOODLES, ETC:

○

TITLE: _____
AUTHOR: _____
ILLUSTRATOR: _____
DATE FINISHED: _____ #PAGES: ____
STORY SHARED BY: _____

Did we like it? ☆ ☆ ☆ ☆ ☆
NOTES, DOODLES, ETC:

○

TITLE: _____

AUTHOR: _____

ILLUSTRATOR: _____

DATE FINISHED: _____ # PAGES: ___

STORY SHARED BY: _____

DID WE LIKE IT? ☆ ☆ ☆ ☆ ☆

NOTES, DOODLES, ETC:

TITLE: _____

AUTHOR: _____

ILLUSTRATOR: _____

DATE FINISHED: _____ # PAGES: ___

STORY SHARED BY: _____

DID WE LIKE IT? ☆ ☆ ☆ ☆ ☆

NOTES, DOODLES, ETC:

"The best of a book
is not the thought
which it contains,
but the thought
which it suggests;
just as the charm of
music dwells not
in the tones
but in the echoes
of our hearts."

— Oliver Wendell Holmes Sr.

TITLE: _____

AUTHOR: _____

ILLUSTRATOR: _____

DATE FINISHED: _____ # PAGES: ___

STORY SHARED BY: _____

DID WE LIKE IT? ☆ ☆ ☆ ☆ ☆

NOTES, DOODLES, ETC:

TITLE: _____
AUTHOR: _____
ILLUSTRATOR: _____
DATE FINISHED: _____ #PAGES: ___
STORY SHARED BY: _____

Did we like it? ☆ ☆ ☆ ☆ ☆
NOTES, DOODLES, ETC:

○

TITLE: _____
AUTHOR: _____
ILLUSTRATOR: _____
DATE FINISHED: _____ #PAGES: ___
STORY SHARED BY: _____

Did we like it? ☆ ☆ ☆ ☆ ☆
NOTES, DOODLES, ETC:

○

TITLE: _____
AUTHOR: _____
ILLUSTRATOR: _____
DATE FINISHED: _____ #PAGES: ___
STORY SHARED BY: _____

Did we like it? ☆ ☆ ☆ ☆ ☆
NOTES, DOODLES, ETC:

○

TITLE: _____
AUTHOR: _____
ILLUSTRATOR: _____
DATE FINISHED: _____ #PAGES: ___
STORY SHARED BY: _____

Did we like it? ☆ ☆ ☆ ☆ ☆
NOTES, DOODLES, ETC:

○

TITLE: _____
AUTHOR: _____
ILLUSTRATOR: _____
DATE FINISHED: _____ #PAGES: ___
STORY SHARED BY: _____

DID WE LIKE IT? ☆ ☆ ☆ ☆ ☆
NOTES, DOODLES, ETC:

TITLE: _____
AUTHOR: _____
ILLUSTRATOR: _____
DATE FINISHED: _____ #PAGES: ___
STORY SHARED BY: _____

DID WE LIKE IT? ☆ ☆ ☆ ☆ ☆
NOTES, DOODLES, ETC:

TITLE: _____
AUTHOR: _____
ILLUSTRATOR: _____
DATE FINISHED: _____ #PAGES: ___
STORY SHARED BY: _____

DID WE LIKE IT? ☆ ☆ ☆ ☆ ☆
NOTES, DOODLES, ETC:

TITLE: _____
AUTHOR: _____
ILLUSTRATOR: _____
DATE FINISHED: _____ #PAGES: ___
STORY SHARED BY: _____

DID WE LIKE IT? ☆ ☆ ☆ ☆ ☆
NOTES, DOODLES, ETC:

TITLE: _____

AUTHOR: _____

ILLUSTRATOR: _____

DATE FINISHED: _____ # PAGES: ____

STORY SHARED BY: _____

_____

DID WE LIKE IT? ☆ ☆ ☆ ☆ ☆

NOTES, DOODLES, ETC:

○

TITLE: _____

AUTHOR: _____

ILLUSTRATOR: _____

DATE FINISHED: _____ # PAGES: ____

STORY SHARED BY: _____

_____

DID WE LIKE IT? ☆ ☆ ☆ ☆ ☆

NOTES, DOODLES, ETC:

○

TITLE: _____

AUTHOR: _____

ILLUSTRATOR: _____

DATE FINISHED: _____ # PAGES: ____

STORY SHARED BY: _____

_____

DID WE LIKE IT? ☆ ☆ ☆ ☆ ☆

NOTES, DOODLES, ETC:

○

TITLE: _____

AUTHOR: _____

ILLUSTRATOR: _____

DATE FINISHED: _____ # PAGES: ____

STORY SHARED BY: _____

_____

DID WE LIKE IT? ☆ ☆ ☆ ☆ ☆

NOTES, DOODLES, ETC:

○

TITLE: _____
AUTHOR: _____
ILLUSTRATOR: _____
DATE FINISHED: _____ # PAGES: ___
STORY SHARED BY: _____

Did we like it? ☆ ☆ ☆ ☆ ☆
NOTES, DOODLES, ETC:

"I have never
let my schooling
interfere
with my education."

— Grant Allen

TITLE: _____
AUTHOR: _____
ILLUSTRATOR: _____
DATE FINISHED: _____ # PAGES: ___
STORY SHARED BY: _____

Did we like it? ☆ ☆ ☆ ☆ ☆
NOTES, DOODLES, ETC:

TITLE: _____
AUTHOR: _____
ILLUSTRATOR: _____
DATE FINISHED: _____ # PAGES: ___
STORY SHARED BY: _____

Did we like it? ☆ ☆ ☆ ☆ ☆
NOTES, DOODLES, ETC:

TITLE: _____
AUTHOR: _____
ILLUSTRATOR: _____
DATE FINISHED: _____ #PAGES: ___
STORY SHARED BY: _____

DID WE LIKE IT?   ☆ ☆ ☆ ☆ ☆
NOTES, DOODLES, ETC:

TITLE: _____
AUTHOR: _____
ILLUSTRATOR: _____
DATE FINISHED: _____ #PAGES: ___
STORY SHARED BY: _____

DID WE LIKE IT?   ☆ ☆ ☆ ☆ ☆
NOTES, DOODLES, ETC:

TITLE: _____
AUTHOR: _____
ILLUSTRATOR: _____
DATE FINISHED: _____ #PAGES: ___
STORY SHARED BY: _____

DID WE LIKE IT?   ☆ ☆ ☆ ☆ ☆
NOTES, DOODLES, ETC:

TITLE: _____
AUTHOR: _____
ILLUSTRATOR: _____
DATE FINISHED: _____ #PAGES: ___
STORY SHARED BY: _____

DID WE LIKE IT?   ☆ ☆ ☆ ☆ ☆
NOTES, DOODLES, ETC:

TITLE: _____
AUTHOR: _____
ILLUSTRATOR: _____
DATE FINISHED: _____ #PAGES:___
STORY SHARED BY: _____
_____

DID WE LIKE IT? ☆ ☆ ☆ ☆ ☆
NOTES, DOODLES, ETC:

○

TITLE: _____
AUTHOR: _____
ILLUSTRATOR: _____
DATE FINISHED: _____ #PAGES:___
STORY SHARED BY: _____
_____

DID WE LIKE IT? ☆ ☆ ☆ ☆ ☆
NOTES, DOODLES, ETC:

○

TITLE: _____
AUTHOR: _____
ILLUSTRATOR: _____
DATE FINISHED: _____ #PAGES:___
STORY SHARED BY: _____
_____

DID WE LIKE IT? ☆ ☆ ☆ ☆ ☆
NOTES, DOODLES, ETC:

○

TITLE: _____
AUTHOR: _____
ILLUSTRATOR: _____
DATE FINISHED: _____ #PAGES:___
STORY SHARED BY: _____
_____

DID WE LIKE IT? ☆ ☆ ☆ ☆ ☆
NOTES, DOODLES, ETC:

○

TITLE: _____
AUTHOR: _____
ILLUSTRATOR: _____
DATE FINISHED: _____ #PAGES: ____
STORY SHARED BY: _____

Did we like it? ☆ ☆ ☆ ☆ ☆
NOTES, DOODLES, ETC:

TITLE: _____
AUTHOR: _____
ILLUSTRATOR: _____
DATE FINISHED: _____ #PAGES: ____
STORY SHARED BY: _____

Did we like it? ☆ ☆ ☆ ☆ ☆
NOTES, DOODLES, ETC:

TITLE: _____
AUTHOR: _____
ILLUSTRATOR: _____
DATE FINISHED: _____ #PAGES: ____
STORY SHARED BY: _____

Did we like it? ☆ ☆ ☆ ☆ ☆
NOTES, DOODLES, ETC:

TITLE: _____

AUTHOR: _____

ILLUSTRATOR: _____

DATE FINISHED: _____ # PAGES: ___

STORY SHARED BY: _____

Did we like it? ☆ ☆ ☆ ☆ ☆

NOTES, DOODLES, ETC:

TITLE: _____

AUTHOR: _____

ILLUSTRATOR: _____

DATE FINISHED: _____ # PAGES: ___

STORY SHARED BY: _____

Did we like it? ☆ ☆ ☆ ☆ ☆

NOTES, DOODLES, ETC:

TITLE: _____

AUTHOR: _____

ILLUSTRATOR: _____

DATE FINISHED: _____ # PAGES: ___

STORY SHARED BY: _____

Did we like it? ☆ ☆ ☆ ☆ ☆

NOTES, DOODLES, ETC:

TITLE: _____

AUTHOR: _____

ILLUSTRATOR: _____

DATE FINISHED: _____ # PAGES: ___

STORY SHARED BY: _____

Did we like it? ☆ ☆ ☆ ☆ ☆

NOTES, DOODLES, ETC:

TITLE: _____
AUTHOR: _____
ILLUSTRATOR: _____
DATE FINISHED: _____ #PAGES: ___
STORY SHARED BY: _____

Did we like it? ☆ ☆ ☆ ☆ ☆
NOTES, DOODLES, ETC:

TITLE: _____
AUTHOR: _____
ILLUSTRATOR: _____
DATE FINISHED: _____ #PAGES: __
STORY SHARED BY: _____

Did we like it? ☆ ☆ ☆ ☆ ☆
NOTES, DOODLES, ETC:

TITLE: _____
AUTHOR: _____
ILLUSTRATOR: _____
DATE FINISHED: _____ #PAGES: __
STORY SHARED BY: _____

Did we like it? ☆ ☆ ☆ ☆ ☆
NOTES, DOODLES, ETC:

TITLE: _____
AUTHOR: _____
ILLUSTRATOR: _____
DATE FINISHED: _____ #PAGES: __
STORY SHARED BY: _____

Did we like it? ☆ ☆ ☆ ☆ ☆
NOTES, DOODLES, ETC:

TITLE: _____
AUTHOR: _____
ILLUSTRATOR: _____
DATE FINISHED: _____ # PAGES: ___
STORY SHARED BY: _____

Did we like it?   ☆ ☆ ☆ ☆ ☆
NOTES, DOODLES, ETC:

○

TITLE: _____
AUTHOR: _____
ILLUSTRATOR: _____
DATE FINISHED: _____ # PAGES: ___
STORY SHARED BY: _____

Did we like it?   ☆ ☆ ☆ ☆ ☆
NOTES, DOODLES, ETC:

○

TITLE: _____
AUTHOR: _____
ILLUSTRATOR: _____
DATE FINISHED: _____ # PAGES: ___
STORY SHARED BY: _____

Did we like it?   ☆ ☆ ☆ ☆ ☆
NOTES, DOODLES, ETC:

○

"Life itself is the most wonderful fairytale.

— Hans Christian Andersen

TITLE: _____
AUTHOR: _____
ILLUSTRATOR: _____
DATE FINISHED: _____ #PAGES: ___
STORY SHARED BY: _____

Did we like it?   ☆ ☆ ☆ ☆ ☆
NOTES, DOODLES, ETC:

○

TITLE: _____
AUTHOR: _____
ILLUSTRATOR: _____
DATE FINISHED: _____ #PAGES: ___
STORY SHARED BY: _____

Did we like it?   ☆ ☆ ☆ ☆ ☆
NOTES, DOODLES, ETC:

○

TITLE: _____
AUTHOR: _____
ILLUSTRATOR: _____
DATE FINISHED: _____ #PAGES: ___
STORY SHARED BY: _____

Did we like it?   ☆ ☆ ☆ ☆ ☆
NOTES, DOODLES, ETC:

○

TITLE: _____
AUTHOR: _____
ILLUSTRATOR: _____
DATE FINISHED: _____ #PAGES: ___
STORY SHARED BY: _____

Did we like it?   ☆ ☆ ☆ ☆ ☆
NOTES, DOODLES, ETC:

○

TITLE: _____
AUTHOR: _____
ILLUSTRATOR: _____
DATE FINISHED: _____ # PAGES: ___
STORY SHARED BY: _____

DID WE LIKE IT? ☆ ☆ ☆ ☆ ☆
NOTES, DOODLES, ETC:

"Don't you
    just love poetry
  that gives you
    a crinkly feeling
  up and down
    your back?"

— L.M. Montgomery, **Anne of Green Gables**

TITLE: _____
AUTHOR: _____
ILLUSTRATOR: _____
DATE FINISHED: _____ # PAGES: ___
STORY SHARED BY: _____

DID WE LIKE IT? ☆ ☆ ☆ ☆ ☆
NOTES, DOODLES, ETC:

TITLE: _____
AUTHOR: _____
ILLUSTRATOR: _____
DATE FINISHED: _____ # PAGES: ___
STORY SHARED BY: _____

DID WE LIKE IT? ☆ ☆ ☆ ☆ ☆
NOTES, DOODLES, ETC:

TITLE: _____

AUTHOR: _____

ILLUSTRATOR: _____

DATE FINISHED: _____ #PAGES: ____

STORY SHARED BY: _____

_____

DID WE LIKE IT? ☆ ☆ ☆ ☆ ☆

NOTES, DOODLES, ETC:

○

TITLE: _____

AUTHOR: _____

ILLUSTRATOR: _____

DATE FINISHED: _____ #PAGES: ___

STORY SHARED BY: _____

_____

DID WE LIKE IT? ☆ ☆ ☆ ☆ ☆

NOTES, DOODLES, ETC:

○

TITLE: _____

AUTHOR: _____

ILLUSTRATOR: _____

DATE FINISHED: _____ #PAGES: __

STORY SHARED BY: _____

_____

DID WE LIKE IT? ☆ ☆ ☆ ☆ ☆

NOTES, DOODLES, ETC:

○

TITLE: _____

AUTHOR: _____

ILLUSTRATOR: _____

DATE FINISHED: _____ #PAGES: __

STORY SHARED BY: _____

_____

DID WE LIKE IT? ☆ ☆ ☆ ☆ ☆

NOTES, DOODLES, ETC:

○

TITLE: _____

AUTHOR: _____

ILLUSTRATOR: _____

DATE FINISHED: _____ #PAGES: ___

STORY SHARED BY: _____

Did we like it? ☆ ☆ ☆ ☆ ☆

NOTES, DOODLES, ETC:

TITLE: _____

AUTHOR: _____

ILLUSTRATOR: _____

DATE FINISHED: _____ #PAGES: ___

STORY SHARED BY: _____

Did we like it? ☆ ☆ ☆ ☆ ☆

NOTES, DOODLES, ETC:

TITLE: _____

AUTHOR: _____

ILLUSTRATOR: _____

DATE FINISHED: _____ #PAGES: ___

STORY SHARED BY: _____

Did we like it? ☆ ☆ ☆ ☆ ☆

NOTES, DOODLES, ETC:

TITLE: _____

AUTHOR: _____

ILLUSTRATOR: _____

DATE FINISHED: _____ #PAGES: ___

STORY SHARED BY: _____

Did we like it? ☆ ☆ ☆ ☆ ☆

NOTES, DOODLES, ETC:

TITLE: _____
AUTHOR: _____
ILLUSTRATOR: _____
DATE FINISHED: _____ # PAGES: ___
STORY SHARED BY: _____

Did we like it? ☆ ☆ ☆ ☆ ☆
NOTES, DOODLES, ETC:

TITLE: _____
AUTHOR: _____
ILLUSTRATOR: _____
DATE FINISHED: _____ # PAGES: ___
STORY SHARED BY: _____

Did we like it? ☆ ☆ ☆ ☆ ☆
NOTES, DOODLES, ETC:

TITLE: _____
AUTHOR: _____
ILLUSTRATOR: _____
DATE FINISHED: _____ # PAGES: ___
STORY SHARED BY: _____

Did we like it? ☆ ☆ ☆ ☆ ☆
NOTES, DOODLES, ETC:

TITLE: _____
AUTHOR: _____
ILLUSTRATOR: _____
DATE FINISHED: _____ # PAGES: ___
STORY SHARED BY: _____

Did we like it? ☆ ☆ ☆ ☆ ☆
NOTES, DOODLES, ETC:

TITLE: _____

AUTHOR: _____

ILLUSTRATOR: _____

DATE FINISHED: _____ #PAGES: ___

STORY SHARED BY: _____

Did we like it? ☆ ☆ ☆ ☆ ☆

NOTES, DOODLES, ETC:

○

TITLE: _____

AUTHOR: _____

ILLUSTRATOR: _____

DATE FINISHED: _____ #PAGES: ___

STORY SHARED BY: _____

Did we like it? ☆ ☆ ☆ ☆ ☆

NOTES, DOODLES, ETC:

○

TITLE: _____

AUTHOR: _____

ILLUSTRATOR: _____

DATE FINISHED: _____ #PAGES: ___

STORY SHARED BY: _____

Did we like it? ☆ ☆ ☆ ☆ ☆

NOTES, DOODLES, ETC:

○

TITLE: _____
AUTHOR: _____
ILLUSTRATOR: _____
DATE FINISHED: _____ #PAGES: ___
STORY SHARED BY: _____
_____
DID WE LIKE IT?   ☆ ☆ ☆ ☆ ☆
NOTES, DOODLES, ETC:

TITLE: _____
AUTHOR: _____
ILLUSTRATOR: _____
DATE FINISHED: _____ #PAGES: ___
STORY SHARED BY: _____
_____
DID WE LIKE IT?   ☆ ☆ ☆ ☆ ☆
NOTES, DOODLES, ETC:

TITLE: _____
AUTHOR: _____
ILLUSTRATOR: _____
DATE FINISHED: _____ #PAGES: ___
STORY SHARED BY: _____
_____
DID WE LIKE IT?   ☆ ☆ ☆ ☆ ☆
NOTES, DOODLES, ETC:

TITLE: _____
AUTHOR: _____
ILLUSTRATOR: _____
DATE FINISHED: _____ #PAGES: ___
STORY SHARED BY: _____
_____
DID WE LIKE IT?   ☆ ☆ ☆ ☆ ☆
NOTES, DOODLES, ETC:

107

TITLE: _____

AUTHOR: _____

ILLUSTRATOR: _____

DATE FINISHED: _____ # PAGES: ____

STORY SHARED BY: _____

Did we like it? ☆ ☆ ☆ ☆ ☆

NOTES, DOODLES, ETC:

TITLE: _____

AUTHOR: _____

ILLUSTRATOR: _____

DATE FINISHED: _____ # PAGES: ____

STORY SHARED BY: _____

Did we like it? ☆ ☆ ☆ ☆ ☆

NOTES, DOODLES, ETC:

TITLE: _____

AUTHOR: _____

ILLUSTRATOR: _____

DATE FINISHED: _____ # PAGES: ____

STORY SHARED BY: _____

Did we like it? ☆ ☆ ☆ ☆ ☆

NOTES, DOODLES, ETC:

TITLE: _____

AUTHOR: _____

ILLUSTRATOR: _____

DATE FINISHED: _____ # PAGES: ____

STORY SHARED BY: _____

Did we like it? ☆ ☆ ☆ ☆ ☆

NOTES, DOODLES, ETC:

"For books are more than books, they are the life, the very heart and core of ages past, the reason why men worked and died, the essence and quintessence of their lives."

— Marcus Tullius Cicero

Title: _____
Author: _____
Illustrator: _____
Date finished: _____ #Pages: ___
Story shared by: _____

Did we like it? ☆☆☆☆☆
Notes, doodles, etc:

Title: _____
Author: _____
Illustrator: _____
Date finished: _____ #Pages: ___
Story shared by: _____

Did we like it? ☆☆☆☆☆
Notes, doodles, etc:

Title: _____
Author: _____
Illustrator: _____
Date finished: _____ #Pages: ___
Story shared by: _____

Did we like it? ☆☆☆☆☆
Notes, doodles, etc:

TITLE: _____
AUTHOR: _____
ILLUSTRATOR: _____
DATE FINISHED: _____ #PAGES:____
STORY SHARED BY: _____
_____
DID WE LIKE IT?   ☆ ☆ ☆ ☆ ☆
NOTES, DOODLES, ETC:

○

TITLE: _____
AUTHOR: _____
ILLUSTRATOR: _____
DATE FINISHED: _____ #PAGES:___
STORY SHARED BY: _____
_____
DID WE LIKE IT?   ☆ ☆ ☆ ☆ ☆
NOTES, DOODLES, ETC:

○

TITLE: _____
AUTHOR: _____
ILLUSTRATOR: _____
DATE FINISHED: _____ #PAGES:____
STORY SHARED BY: _____
_____
DID WE LIKE IT?   ☆ ☆ ☆ ☆ ☆
NOTES, DOODLES, ETC:

○

TITLE: _____
AUTHOR: _____
ILLUSTRATOR: _____
DATE FINISHED: _____ #PAGES:___
STORY SHARED BY: _____
_____
DID WE LIKE IT?   ☆ ☆ ☆ ☆ ☆
NOTES, DOODLES, ETC:

○

TITLE: _____

AUTHOR: _____

ILLUSTRATOR: _____

DATE FINISHED: _____ #PAGES: ___

STORY SHARED BY: _____

Did we like it? ☆ ☆ ☆ ☆ ☆

NOTES, DOODLES, ETC:

○

TITLE: _____

AUTHOR: _____

ILLUSTRATOR: _____

DATE FINISHED: _____ #PAGES: ___

STORY SHARED BY: _____

Did we like it? ☆ ☆ ☆ ☆ ☆

NOTES, DOODLES, ETC:

○

TITLE: _____

AUTHOR: _____

ILLUSTRATOR: _____

DATE FINISHED: _____ #PAGES: ___

STORY SHARED BY: _____

Did we like it? ☆ ☆ ☆ ☆ ☆

NOTES, DOODLES, ETC:

○

FEATURE LISTS

FEATURE LISTS are special book journal sections where you can keep track of all your favorite books, characters, quotes, words, and story twists, so you never forget them! It's a good idea to become familiar with all of the FEATURE LISTS before you even start writing in the journal. That way you'll know what sorts of things to look for on your reading adventures.

NOTE: When you're filling out a FEATURE LIST form, you'll see spaces to write the JEP#. That's short for "Journal Entry Page #." That just means the page number in the main journal section of *Stories We Shared* where you recorded that book's information. When you fill in a FEATURE LIST, you won't record as much information as you do in the main journal section. Writing down the book's JEP# on the FEATURE LIST form will give you a quick way to cross-reference the title.

New Words We Like!. . . . . . . PG 111
Our Favorite Quotes . . . . PG 123
Most Memorable Characters . . PG 135
Most Surprising Story Twists. . PG 140
Books That Made Us Laugh . . PG 144
Books That Made Us Cry. . . . PG 148
Books That Changed Us . . . . PG 152
Our Very Favorite Books!. . . . PG 156

NEW WORDS WE LIKE!

"'Words aren't made — they grow,' said Anne."
— L. M. MONTGOMERY, *Anne of the Island*

As you read, you'll meet many new words you've never met before; words like *supercilious* or *opulent* or *fulvous*. Some will be mysterious, some will be serious, some will be odd. Some might even make you laugh out loud when you say them, like *hurdy-gurdy* or *argy-bargy* or *fuddy-duddy* or *gobbledygook*. (Yes, those are all real words!)

The thing to remember is that words are like beads. You string beads together to make a necklace. You string words together to build an idea. Each word means something, and when you put words together you're building some new idea that you can then share with other people. The more words you know, the more ideas you'll be able to understand and express. The more words you know, the more things you can think about!

So collect as many words as you can in your life.

This page and the several that follow are places for you to write down new words as you encounter them in books and stories. When you "meet" an interesting word for the first time, politely ask the reader to pause so that you can write the new word in this list. You will probably want to look up the definition or ask someone what it means, and then write the definition beside the word. Afterwards, try to think up a sentence that uses your new word. Using a new word in a sentence will help you remember it.

Learn as many words as you can, so that you can think deeper and deeper thoughts and express more and more thoughtful ideas.

Become a lifelong word-collector!

WORD:_____ DEFINITION:_____

_____

BOOK DISCOVERED IN:_____ JEP#:_____

WORD:_____ DEFINITION:_____

_____

BOOK DISCOVERED IN:_____ JEP#:_____

WORD:_____ DEFINITION:_____

_____

BOOK DISCOVERED IN:_____ JEP#:_____

WORD:_____ DEFINITION:_____

_____

BOOK DISCOVERED IN:_____ JEP#:_____

WORD:_____ DEFINITION:_____

_____

BOOK DISCOVERED IN:_____ JEP#:_____

WORD:_____ DEFINITION:_____

_____

BOOK DISCOVERED IN:_____ JEP#:_____

WORD:_____ DEFINITION:_____

_____

BOOK DISCOVERED IN:_____ JEP#:_____

WORD:_____ DEFINITION:_____

_____

BOOK DISCOVERED IN:_____ JEP#:_____

WORD:_____ DEFINITION:_____

_____

BOOK DISCOVERED IN:_____ JEP#:_____

WORD:_____ DEFINITION:_____

_____

BOOK DISCOVERED IN:_____ JEP#:_____

WORD:_____ DEFINITION:_____

_____

BOOK DISCOVERED IN:_____ JEP#:_____

WORD:_____ DEFINITION:_____

_____

BOOK DISCOVERED IN:_____ JEP#:_____

WORD:_____ DEFINITION:_____

_____

BOOK DISCOVERED IN:_____ JEP#:_____

WORD:_____ DEFINITION:_____

_____

BOOK DISCOVERED IN:_____ JEP#:_____

WORD:_____ DEFINITION:_____

_____

BOOK DISCOVERED IN:_____ JEP#:_____

WORD:_____ DEFINITION:_____

_____

BOOK DISCOVERED IN:_____ JEP#:_____

WORD:_____ DEFINITION:_____

_____

BOOK DISCOVERED IN:_____ JEP#:_____

WORD:_____ DEFINITION:_____

_____

BOOK DISCOVERED IN:_____ JEP#:_____

WORD:_____ DEFINITION:_____

_____

BOOK DISCOVERED IN:_____ JEP#:_____

WORD:_____ DEFINITION:_____

_____

BOOK DISCOVERED IN:_____ JEP#:_____

WORD:_____ DEFINITION:_____

_____

BOOK DISCOVERED IN:_____ JEP#:_____

WORD:_____ DEFINITION:_____

_____

BOOK DISCOVERED IN:_____ JEP#:_____

WORD:_____ DEFINITION:_____

_____

BOOK DISCOVERED IN:_____ JEP#:_____

WORD:_____ DEFINITION:_____

_____

BOOK DISCOVERED IN:_____ JEP#:_____

WORD:_____ DEFINITION:_____

_____

BOOK DISCOVERED IN:_____ JEP#:_____

WORD:_____ DEFINITION:_____

_____

BOOK DISCOVERED IN:_____ JEP#:_____

WORD:_____ DEFINITION:_____

_____

BOOK DISCOVERED IN:_____ JEP#:_____

WORD:_____ DEFINITION:_____

_____

BOOK DISCOVERED IN:_____ JEP#:_____

WORD:_____ DEFINITION:_____

_____

BOOK DISCOVERED IN:_____ JEP#:_____

WORD:_____ DEFINITION:_____

_____

BOOK DISCOVERED IN:_____ JEP#:_____

WORD:_____ DEFINITION:_____

_____

BOOK DISCOVERED IN:_____ JEP#:_____

WORD:_____ DEFINITION:_____

_____

BOOK DISCOVERED IN:_____ JEP#:_____

WORD:_____ DEFINITION:_____

_____

BOOK DISCOVERED IN:_____ JEP#:_____

WORD:_____ DEFINITION:_____

_____

BOOK DISCOVERED IN:_____ JEP#:_____

WORD:_____ DEFINITION:_____

_____

BOOK DISCOVERED IN:_____ JEP#:_____

WORD:_____ DEFINITION:_____

_____

BOOK DISCOVERED IN:_____ JEP#:_____

WORD:_____ DEFINITION:_____

_____

BOOK DISCOVERED IN:_____ JEP#:_____

WORD:_____ DEFINITION:_____

_____

BOOK DISCOVERED IN:_____ JEP#:_____

WORD:_____ DEFINITION:_____

_____

BOOK DISCOVERED IN:_____ JEP#:_____

WORD:_____ DEFINITION:_____

_____

BOOK DISCOVERED IN:_____ JEP#:_____

WORD:_____ DEFINITION:_____

_____

BOOK DISCOVERED IN:_____ JEP#:_____

WORD:_____ DEFINITION:_____

_____

BOOK DISCOVERED IN:_____ JEP#:_____

WORD:_____ DEFINITION:_____

_____

BOOK DISCOVERED IN:_____ JEP#:_____

WORD:_____ DEFINITION:_____

_____

BOOK DISCOVERED IN:_____ JEP#:_____

WORD:_____ DEFINITION:_____

_____

BOOK DISCOVERED IN:_____ JEP#:_____

WORD:_____ DEFINITION:_____

_____

BOOK DISCOVERED IN:_____ JEP#:_____

WORD:_____ DEFINITION:_____

_____

BOOK DISCOVERED IN:_____ JEP#:_____

WORD:_____ DEFINITION:_____

_____

BOOK DISCOVERED IN:_____ JEP#:_____

WORD:_____ DEFINITION:_____

_____

BOOK DISCOVERED IN:_____ JEP#:_____

WORD:_____ DEFINITION:_____

_____

BOOK DISCOVERED IN:_____ JEP#:_____

WORD:_____ DEFINITION:_____
_____
BOOK DISCOVERED IN:_____ JEP#:_____

WORD:_____ DEFINITION:_____
_____
BOOK DISCOVERED IN:_____ JEP#:_____

WORD:_____ DEFINITION:_____
_____
BOOK DISCOVERED IN:_____ JEP#:_____

WORD:_____ DEFINITION:_____
_____
BOOK DISCOVERED IN:_____ JEP#:_____

WORD:_____ DEFINITION:_____
_____
BOOK DISCOVERED IN:_____ JEP#:_____

WORD:_____ DEFINITION:_____
_____
BOOK DISCOVERED IN:_____ JEP#:_____

WORD:_____ DEFINITION:_____
_____
BOOK DISCOVERED IN:_____ JEP#:_____

WORD:_____ DEFINITION:_____
_____
BOOK DISCOVERED IN:_____ JEP#:_____

WORD:_____ DEFINITION:_____
_____
BOOK DISCOVERED IN:_____ JEP#:_____

WORD:_____ DEFINITION:_____
_____
BOOK DISCOVERED IN:_____ JEP#:_____
WORD:_____ DEFINITION:_____
_____
BOOK DISCOVERED IN:_____ JEP#:_____
WORD:_____ DEFINITION:_____
_____
BOOK DISCOVERED IN:_____ JEP#:_____
WORD:_____ DEFINITION:_____
_____
BOOK DISCOVERED IN:_____ JEP#:_____
WORD:_____ DEFINITION:_____
_____
BOOK DISCOVERED IN:_____ JEP#:_____
WORD:_____ DEFINITION:_____
_____
BOOK DISCOVERED IN:_____ JEP#:_____
WORD:_____ DEFINITION:_____
_____
BOOK DISCOVERED IN:_____ JEP#:_____
WORD:_____ DEFINITION:_____
_____
BOOK DISCOVERED IN:_____ JEP#:_____
WORD:_____ DEFINITION:_____
_____
BOOK DISCOVERED IN:_____ JEP#:_____

WORD:_____ DEFINITION:_____

_____

BOOK DISCOVERED IN:_____ JEP#:_____

WORD:_____ DEFINITION:_____

_____

BOOK DISCOVERED IN:_____ JEP#:_____

WORD:_____ DEFINITION:_____

_____

BOOK DISCOVERED IN:_____ JEP#:_____

WORD:_____ DEFINITION:_____

_____

BOOK DISCOVERED IN:_____ JEP#:_____

WORD:_____ DEFINITION:_____

_____

BOOK DISCOVERED IN:_____ JEP#:_____

WORD:_____ DEFINITION:_____

_____

BOOK DISCOVERED IN:_____ JEP#:_____

WORD:_____ DEFINITION:_____

_____

BOOK DISCOVERED IN:_____ JEP#:_____

WORD:_____ DEFINITION:_____

_____

BOOK DISCOVERED IN:_____ JEP#:_____

OUR FAVORITE QUOTES

"The worth of a book is to be measured by what
you can carry away from it."
— JAMES BRYCE

Sometimes an author creates a sentence or a paragraph so meaningful, beautiful and moving that you will want to ask the reader to stop and read that part of the story again. Some sentences, you'll want to remember for the rest of your life. This is where you can write down those favorite quotes you find in stories, so you can read them again and again over the years. A few might even be wonderful enough you'll want to memorize them, so they'll be fixed in your imagination forever!

QUOTE: _____

_____

_____

_____ AUTHOR: _____

BOOK TITLE: _____ JEP#: _____

QUOTE: _____

_____

_____

_____ AUTHOR: _____

BOOK TITLE: _____ JEP#: _____

QUOTE: _____

_____

_____

_____ AUTHOR: _____

BOOK TITLE: _____ JEP#: _____

QUOTE: _____

_____

_____

_____ AUTHOR: _____

BOOK TITLE: _____ JEP#: _____

_____ AUTHOR: _____

BOOK TITLE: _____ JEP#: _____

QUOTE: _____

_____

_____

_____ AUTHOR: _____

BOOK TITLE: _____ JEP#: _____

QUOTE: _____

_____

_____ AUTHOR: _____

BOOK TITLE: _____ JEP#: _____

QUOTE: _____

_____

_____ AUTHOR: _____

BOOK TITLE: _____ JEP#: _____

QUOTE: _____

_____

_____ AUTHOR: _____

BOOK TITLE: _____ JEP#: _____

QUOTE: _____

_____

_____ AUTHOR: _____

BOOK TITLE: _____ JEP#: _____

_____ AUTHOR: _____

BOOK TITLE: _____ JEP#: _____

QUOTE: _____

_____

_____

_____ AUTHOR:_____

BOOK TITLE:_____ JEP#:_____

QUOTE: _____

_____

_____ AUTHOR:_____

BOOK TITLE:_____ JEP#:_____

QUOTE: _____

_____

_____ AUTHOR:_____

BOOK TITLE:_____ JEP#:_____

QUOTE: _____

_____

_____ AUTHOR:_____

BOOK TITLE:_____ JEP#:_____

QUOTE: _____

_____

_____ AUTHOR:_____

BOOK TITLE:_____ JEP#:_____

_____ AUTHOR:_____

BOOK TITLE:_____ JEP#:_____

QUOTE: _____

_____

_____

_____ AUTHOR: _____

BOOK TITLE: _____ JEP#: _____

QUOTE: _____

_____

_____

_____ AUTHOR: _____

BOOK TITLE: _____ JEP#: _____

QUOTE: _____

_____

_____

_____ AUTHOR: _____

BOOK TITLE: _____ JEP#: _____

QUOTE: _____

_____

_____

_____ AUTHOR: _____

BOOK TITLE: _____ JEP#: _____

QUOTE: _____

_____

_____

_____ AUTHOR: _____

BOOK TITLE: _____ JEP#: _____

QUOTE: _____

_____

_____

_____ AUTHOR: _____

BOOK TITLE: _____ JEP#: _____

QUOTE: _____

_____

_____

_____ AUTHOR: _____

BOOK TITLE: _____ JEP#: _____

QUOTE: _____

_____

_____

_____ AUTHOR: _____

BOOK TITLE: _____ JEP#: _____

QUOTE: _____

_____

_____

_____ AUTHOR: _____

BOOK TITLE: _____ JEP#: _____

QUOTE: _____

_____

_____

_____ AUTHOR: _____

BOOK TITLE: _____ JEP#: _____

QUOTE: _____

_____

_____

_____ AUTHOR: _____

BOOK TITLE: _____ JEP#: _____

QUOTE: _____

_____

_____

_____ AUTHOR: _____

BOOK TITLE: _____ JEP#: _____

QUOTE: _____

_____

_____

_____ AUTHOR: _____

BOOK TITLE: _____ JEP#: _____

QUOTE: _____

_____

_____

_____ AUTHOR: _____

BOOK TITLE: _____ JEP#: _____

QUOTE: _____

_____

_____

_____ AUTHOR: _____

BOOK TITLE: _____ JEP#: _____

QUOTE: _____

_____

_____

_____ AUTHOR: _____

BOOK TITLE: _____ JEP#: _____

QUOTE: _____

_____

_____

_____ AUTHOR: _____

BOOK TITLE: _____ JEP#: _____

QUOTE: _____

_____

_____

_____ AUTHOR: _____

BOOK TITLE: _____ JEP#: _____

QUOTE: _____

_____

_____

_____ AUTHOR: _____

BOOK TITLE: _____ JEP#: _____

QUOTE: _____

_____

_____

_____ AUTHOR: _____

BOOK TITLE: _____ JEP#: _____

QUOTE: _____

_____

_____

_____ AUTHOR: _____

BOOK TITLE: _____ JEP#: _____

QUOTE: _____

_____

_____ AUTHOR: _____

BOOK TITLE: _____ JEP#: _____

QUOTE: _____

_____

_____ AUTHOR: _____

BOOK TITLE: _____ JEP#: _____

QUOTE: _____

_____

_____ AUTHOR: _____

BOOK TITLE: _____ JEP#: _____

QUOTE: _____

_____

_____ AUTHOR: _____

BOOK TITLE: _____ JEP#: _____

QUOTE: _____

_____

_____ AUTHOR: _____

BOOK TITLE: _____ JEP#: _____

QUOTE: _____

_____

_____

_____ AUTHOR: _____

BOOK TITLE: _____ JEP#: _____

QUOTE: _____

_____

_____

_____ AUTHOR: _____

BOOK TITLE: _____ JEP#: _____

QUOTE: _____

_____

_____

_____ AUTHOR: _____

BOOK TITLE: _____ JEP#: _____

QUOTE: _____

_____

_____

_____ AUTHOR: _____

BOOK TITLE: _____ JEP#: _____

QUOTE: _____

_____

_____

_____ AUTHOR: _____

BOOK TITLE: _____ JEP#: _____

QUOTE: _____

_____

_____

_____ AUTHOR: _____

BOOK TITLE: _____ JEP#: _____

QUOTE: _____

_____

_____

_____ AUTHOR: _____

BOOK TITLE: _____ JEP#: _____

QUOTE: _____

_____

_____

_____ AUTHOR: _____

BOOK TITLE: _____ JEP#: _____

QUOTE: _____

_____

_____

_____ AUTHOR: _____

BOOK TITLE: _____ JEP#: _____

QUOTE: _____

_____

_____

_____ AUTHOR: _____

BOOK TITLE: _____ JEP#: _____

QUOTE: _____

_____

_____

_____ AUTHOR: _____

BOOK TITLE: _____ JEP#: _____

QUOTE: _____

_____

_____ AUTHOR: _____

BOOK TITLE: _____ JEP#: _____

QUOTE: _____

_____

_____ AUTHOR: _____

BOOK TITLE: _____ JEP#: _____

QUOTE: _____

_____

_____ AUTHOR: _____

BOOK TITLE: _____ JEP#: _____

QUOTE: _____

_____

_____ AUTHOR: _____

BOOK TITLE: _____ JEP#: _____

QUOTE: _____

_____

_____

_____ AUTHOR: _____

BOOK TITLE: _____ JEP#: _____

QUOTE: _____

_____

_____

_____ AUTHOR: _____

BOOK TITLE: _____ JEP#: _____

QUOTE: _____

_____

_____

_____ AUTHOR: _____

BOOK TITLE: _____ JEP#: _____

QUOTE: _____

_____

_____

_____ AUTHOR: _____

BOOK TITLE: _____ JEP#: _____

QUOTE: _____

_____

_____

_____ AUTHOR: _____

BOOK TITLE: _____ JEP#: _____

MOST MEMORABLE CHARACTERS

"I wish we could sometimes love the characters in real life as we love the characters in romances. There are a great many human souls whom we should accept more kindly, and even appreciate more clearly, if we simply thought of them as people in a story." — G. K. CHESTERTON, "What I Saw in America"

Authors don't just create stories. They also create characters to live inside those stories. It's the author's job to imagine every important thing about their characters. What do they look like? How do they dress? How do they talk? What sorts of personalities do they have? What do they love? What time period and what part of the world do they live in? What are their likes and dislikes? What are they afraid of?

Some characters are so well written that when you finish a book you'll feel like you've made a new friend. Others might be well-crafted characters who are so villainous you'll be certain you would never want to know them! This list is a place to make note of the most memorable characters you encounter in stories.

Were they extremely clever, heroic, interesting, likeable, treacherous, resilient, or funny? A character you admire? A character you would be best friends with? A character you would never want to run into in a dark alley? Make a list here of all those well-written characters you never want to forget.

CHARACTER:_____ BOOK TITLE:_____
WHY MEMORABLE?:_____
_____ JEP#:_____

CHARACTER:_____ BOOK TITLE:_____
WHY MEMORABLE?:_____
_____ JEP#:_____

CHARACTER:_____ BOOK TITLE:_____
WHY MEMORABLE?:_____
_____ JEP#:_____

CHARACTER:_____ BOOK TITLE:_____
WHY MEMORABLE?:_____
_____ JEP#:_____

CHARACTER:_____ BOOK TITLE:_____
WHY MEMORABLE?:_____
_____ JEP#:_____

CHARACTER:_____ BOOK TITLE:_____
WHY MEMORABLE?:_____
_____ JEP#:_____

CHARACTER:_____ BOOK TITLE:_____
WHY MEMORABLE?:_____
_____ JEP#:_____

CHARACTER:_____ BOOK TITLE:_____
WHY MEMORABLE?:_____
_____ JEP#:_____

CHARACTER:_____ BOOK TITLE:_____
WHY MEMORABLE?:_____
_____ JEP#:_____

CHARACTER:_____ BOOK TITLE:_____
WHY MEMORABLE?:_____
_____ JEP#:_____

CHARACTER:_____ BOOK TITLE:_____
WHY MEMORABLE?:_____
_____ JEP#:_____

CHARACTER:_____ BOOK TITLE:_____
WHY MEMORABLE?:_____
_____ JEP#:_____

CHARACTER:_____ BOOK TITLE:_____
WHY MEMORABLE?:_____
_____ JEP#:_____

CHARACTER:_____ BOOK TITLE:_____
WHY MEMORABLE?:_____
_____ JEP#:_____

CHARACTER:_____ BOOK TITLE:_____
WHY MEMORABLE?:_____
_____ JEP#:_____

CHARACTER:_____ BOOK TITLE:_____
WHY MEMORABLE?:_____
_____ JEP#:_____

CHARACTER:_____ BOOK TITLE:_____
WHY MEMORABLE?:_____
_____ JEP#:_____

CHARACTER:_____ BOOK TITLE:_____
WHY MEMORABLE?:_____
_____ JEP#:_____

CHARACTER:_____ BOOK TITLE:_____
WHY MEMORABLE?:_____
_____ JEP#:_____

CHARACTER:_____ BOOK TITLE:_____
WHY MEMORABLE?:_____
_____ JEP#:_____

CHARACTER:_____ BOOK TITLE:_____
WHY MEMORABLE?:_____
_____ JEP#:_____

CHARACTER:_____ BOOK TITLE:_____
WHY MEMORABLE?:_____
_____ JEP#:_____

CHARACTER:_____ BOOK TITLE:_____
WHY MEMORABLE?:_____
_____ JEP#:_____

CHARACTER:_____ BOOK TITLE:_____
WHY MEMORABLE?:_____
_____ JEP#:_____

CHARACTER:_____ BOOK TITLE:_____
WHY MEMORABLE?:_____
_____ JEP#:_____

CHARACTER:_____ BOOK TITLE:_____
WHY MEMORABLE?:_____
_____ JEP#:_____

CHARACTER:_____ BOOK TITLE:_____
WHY MEMORABLE?:_____
_____ JEP#:_____

CHARACTER:_____ BOOK TITLE:_____
WHY MEMORABLE?:_____
_____ JEP#:_____

CHARACTER:_____ BOOK TITLE:_____
WHY MEMORABLE?:_____
_____ JEP#:_____

CHARACTER:_____ BOOK TITLE:_____
WHY MEMORABLE?:_____
_____ JEP#:_____

CHARACTER:_____ BOOK TITLE:_____
WHY MEMORABLE?:_____
_____ JEP#:_____

CHARACTER:_____ BOOK TITLE:_____
WHY MEMORABLE?:_____
_____ JEP#:_____

CHARACTER:_____ BOOK TITLE:_____
WHY MEMORABLE?:_____
_____ JEP#:_____

CHARACTER:_____ BOOK TITLE:_____
WHY MEMORABLE?:_____
_____ JEP#:_____

CHARACTER:_____ BOOK TITLE:_____
WHY MEMORABLE?:_____
_____ JEP#:_____

CHARACTER:_____ BOOK TITLE:_____
WHY MEMORABLE?:_____
_____ JEP#:_____

CHARACTER:_____ BOOK TITLE:_____
WHY MEMORABLE?:_____
_____ JEP#:_____

CHARACTER:_____ BOOK TITLE:_____
WHY MEMORABLE?:_____
_____ JEP#:_____

CHARACTER:_____ BOOK TITLE:_____
WHY MEMORABLE?:_____
_____ JEP#:_____

CHARACTER:_____ BOOK TITLE:_____
WHY MEMORABLE?:_____
_____ JEP#:_____

CHARACTER:_____ BOOK TITLE:_____
WHY MEMORABLE?:_____
_____ JEP#:_____

CHARACTER:_____ BOOK TITLE:_____
WHY MEMORABLE?:_____
_____ JEP#:_____

CHARACTER:_____ BOOK TITLE:_____
WHY MEMORABLE?:_____
_____ JEP#:_____

CHARACTER:_____ BOOK TITLE:_____
WHY MEMORABLE?:_____
_____ JEP#:_____

CHARACTER:_____ BOOK TITLE:_____
WHY MEMORABLE?:_____
_____ JEP#:_____

CHARACTER:_____ BOOK TITLE:_____
WHY MEMORABLE?:_____
_____ JEP#:_____

CHARACTER:_____ BOOK TITLE:_____
WHY MEMORABLE?:_____
_____ JEP#:_____

CHARACTER:_____ BOOK TITLE:_____
WHY MEMORABLE?:_____
_____ JEP#:_____

CHARACTER:_____ BOOK TITLE:_____
WHY MEMORABLE?:_____
_____ JEP#:_____

CHARACTER:_____ BOOK TITLE:_____
WHY MEMORABLE?:_____
_____ JEP#:_____

MOST SURPRISING STORY TWISTS

"With every step of our lives we enter into the middle of some story
which we are certain to misunderstand."
— G. K. CHESTERTON, *William Blake*

Some stories are predictable. Before you get to the end you already know what's going to happen. Other stories surprise you in amazing ways. You think you know what's going to happen next, and then the plot turns in a way that you never would have guessed. Surprising twists in stories can create some of the most exciting and enjoyable moments for readers. Here's a place where you can record your favorite story twists.

STORY TWIST:_____

_____

BOOK TITLE:_____ JEP#:_____

STORY TWIST:_____

_____

BOOK TITLE:_____ JEP#:_____

STORY TWIST:_____

_____

BOOK TITLE:_____ JEP#:_____

STORY TWIST:_____

_____

BOOK TITLE:_____ JEP#:_____

STORY TWIST:_____

_____

BOOK TITLE:_____ JEP#:_____

STORY TWIST:_____

_____

BOOK TITLE:_____ JEP#:_____

STORY TWIST:_____

_____

BOOK TITLE:_____ JEP#:_____

STORY TWIST:_____

_____

BOOK TITLE:_____ JEP#:_____

STORY TWIST:_____

BOOK TITLE:_____ JEP#:_____
STORY TWIST:_____

BOOK TITLE:_____ JEP#:_____
STORY TWIST:_____

BOOK TITLE:_____ JEP#:_____
STORY TWIST:_____

BOOK TITLE:_____ JEP#:_____
STORY TWIST:_____

BOOK TITLE:_____ JEP#:_____
STORY TWIST:_____

BOOK TITLE:_____ JEP#:_____
STORY TWIST:_____

BOOK TITLE:_____ JEP#:_____
STORY TWIST:_____

BOOK TITLE:_____ JEP#:_____
STORY TWIST:_____

BOOK TITLE:_____ JEP#:_____
STORY TWIST:_____

BOOK TITLE:_____ JEP#:_____

STORY TWIST:_____

BOOK TITLE:_____ JEP#:_____
STORY TWIST:_____

BOOK TITLE:_____ JEP#:_____
STORY TWIST:_____

BOOK TITLE:_____ JEP#:_____
STORY TWIST:_____

BOOK TITLE:_____ JEP#:_____
STORY TWIST:_____

BOOK TITLE:_____ JEP#:_____
STORY TWIST:_____

BOOK TITLE:_____ JEP#:_____
STORY TWIST:_____

BOOK TITLE:_____ JEP#:_____
STORY TWIST:_____

BOOK TITLE:_____ JEP#:_____
STORY TWIST:_____

BOOK TITLE:_____ JEP#:_____
STORY TWIST:_____

BOOK TITLE:_____ JEP#:_____

STORY TWIST:_____

_____

BOOK TITLE:_____ JEP#:_____
STORY TWIST:_____

_____

BOOK TITLE:_____ JEP#:_____
STORY TWIST:_____

_____

BOOK TITLE:_____ JEP#:_____
STORY TWIST:_____

_____

BOOK TITLE:_____ JEP#:_____
STORY TWIST:_____

_____

BOOK TITLE:_____ JEP#:_____
STORY TWIST:_____

_____

BOOK TITLE:_____ JEP#:_____
STORY TWIST:_____

_____

BOOK TITLE:_____ JEP#:_____
STORY TWIST:_____

_____

BOOK TITLE:_____ JEP#:_____
STORY TWIST:_____

_____

BOOK TITLE:_____ JEP#:_____
STORY TWIST:_____

_____

BOOK TITLE:_____ JEP#:_____

BOOKS THAT MADE US LAUGH

"It is one thing to describe an interview with a gorgon or a griffin, a creature who does not exist. It is another thing to discover that the rhinoceros does exist and then take pleasure in the fact that he looks as if he didn't." — G. K. CHESTERTON, *Orthodoxy*

Humor is a powerful tool in the hands of a gifted storyteller. Some stories are funny from start to finish, but even a serious book can have very humorous moments. Why? Because human beings just do and say funny things sometimes! We know in our own lives we can make choices that put us in situations that might not seem funny while we're in the middle of them, but can be hilarious to tell our friends about afterwards. Well, here's a place where you can honor those stories that offered you the gift of laughter. But we're not just talking about a little chuckle or a guffaw. This is a place to memorialize the books that made you laugh so hard you could barely breathe!

WHAT'S SO FUNNY?:_____

_____

BOOK TITLE:_____ JEP#:_____
WHAT'S SO FUNNY?:_____

_____

BOOK TITLE:_____ JEP#:_____
WHAT'S SO FUNNY?:_____

_____

BOOK TITLE:_____ JEP#:_____
WHAT'S SO FUNNY?:_____

_____

BOOK TITLE:_____ JEP#:_____
WHAT'S SO FUNNY?:_____

_____

BOOK TITLE:_____ JEP#:_____
WHAT'S SO FUNNY?:_____

_____

BOOK TITLE:_____ JEP#:_____
WHAT'S SO FUNNY?:_____

_____

BOOK TITLE:_____ JEP#:_____

WHAT'S SO FUNNY?:_____

BOOK TITLE:_____ JEP#:_____
WHAT'S SO FUNNY?:_____

BOOK TITLE:_____ JEP#:_____
WHAT'S SO FUNNY?:_____

BOOK TITLE:_____ JEP#:_____
WHAT'S SO FUNNY?:_____

BOOK TITLE:_____ JEP#:_____
WHAT'S SO FUNNY?:_____

BOOK TITLE:_____ JEP#:_____
WHAT'S SO FUNNY?:_____

BOOK TITLE:_____ JEP#:_____
WHAT'S SO FUNNY?:_____

BOOK TITLE:_____ JEP#:_____
WHAT'S SO FUNNY?:_____

BOOK TITLE:_____ JEP#:_____
WHAT'S SO FUNNY?:_____

BOOK TITLE:_____ JEP#:_____
WHAT'S SO FUNNY?:_____

BOOK TITLE:_____ JEP#:_____

WHAT'S SO FUNNY?:_____

_____

BOOK TITLE:_____ JEP#:_____

WHAT'S SO FUNNY?:_____

_____

BOOK TITLE:_____ JEP#:_____

WHAT'S SO FUNNY?:_____

_____

BOOK TITLE:_____ JEP#:_____

WHAT'S SO FUNNY?:_____

_____

BOOK TITLE:_____ JEP#:_____

WHAT'S SO FUNNY?:_____

_____

BOOK TITLE:_____ JEP#:_____

WHAT'S SO FUNNY?:_____

_____

BOOK TITLE:_____ JEP#:_____

WHAT'S SO FUNNY?:_____

_____

BOOK TITLE:_____ JEP#:_____

WHAT'S SO FUNNY?:_____

_____

BOOK TITLE:_____ JEP#:_____

WHAT'S SO FUNNY?:_____

_____

BOOK TITLE:_____ JEP#:_____

WHAT'S SO FUNNY?:_____

_____

BOOK TITLE:_____ JEP#:_____

WHAT'S SO FUNNY?:_____

_____

BOOK TITLE:_____ JEP#:_____
WHAT'S SO FUNNY?:_____

_____

BOOK TITLE:_____ JEP#:_____
WHAT'S SO FUNNY?:_____

_____

BOOK TITLE:_____ JEP#:_____
WHAT'S SO FUNNY?:_____

_____

BOOK TITLE:_____ JEP#:_____
WHAT'S SO FUNNY?:_____

_____

BOOK TITLE:_____ JEP#:_____
WHAT'S SO FUNNY?:_____

_____

BOOK TITLE:_____ JEP#:_____
WHAT'S SO FUNNY?:_____

_____

BOOK TITLE:_____ JEP#:_____
WHAT'S SO FUNNY?:_____

_____

BOOK TITLE:_____ JEP#:_____
WHAT'S SO FUNNY?:_____

_____

BOOK TITLE:_____ JEP#:_____
WHAT'S SO FUNNY?:_____

_____

BOOK TITLE:_____ JEP#:_____
WHAT'S SO FUNNY?:_____

_____

BOOK TITLE:_____ JEP#:_____

BOOKS THAT MADE US CRY

"Fill your paper with the breathings of your heart."
— WILLIAM WORDSWORTH

Sometimes we're drawn into a story and come to care so much about the characters that when something sad happens to them, the very best thing we can do as human beings is to cry. A great story has the power to make us feel. We journey with the characters we love through good times and bad, through victories and defeats. Did you know that one of the highest compliments an author can receive is to learn that a reader loved the writer's characters so much that the story made them cry? Never be ashamed if a story moves you to tears. It doesn't mean you're weak. It actually means you're strong. You're strong enough to let yourself care about another person (even a person in a story). You're strong enough to feel deep feelings and you're strong enough to show them. Here's the place you can keep track of stories that made you feel something so deeply you were moved to tears.

WHY WE CRIED:_____

_____

BOOK TITLE:_____ JEP#:_____

WHY WE CRIED:_____

_____

BOOK TITLE:_____ JEP#:_____

WHY WE CRIED:_____

_____

BOOK TITLE:_____ JEP#:_____

WHY WE CRIED:_____

_____

BOOK TITLE:_____ JEP#:_____

WHY WE CRIED:_____

_____

BOOK TITLE:_____ JEP#:_____

WHY WE CRIED:_____

_____

BOOK TITLE:_____ JEP#:_____

WHY WE CRIED:_____

_____

BOOK TITLE:_____ JEP#:_____

WHY WE CRIED:_____

_____

BOOK TITLE:_____ JEP#:_____

WHY WE CRIED:_____
_____

BOOK TITLE:_____ JEP#:_____
WHY WE CRIED:_____
_____

BOOK TITLE:_____ JEP#:_____
WHY WE CRIED:_____
_____

BOOK TITLE:_____ JEP#:_____
WHY WE CRIED:_____
_____

BOOK TITLE:_____ JEP#:_____
WHY WE CRIED:_____
_____

BOOK TITLE:_____ JEP#:_____
WHY WE CRIED:_____
_____

BOOK TITLE:_____ JEP#:_____
WHY WE CRIED:_____
_____

BOOK TITLE:_____ JEP#:_____
WHY WE CRIED:_____
_____

BOOK TITLE:_____ JEP#:_____
WHY WE CRIED:_____
_____

BOOK TITLE:_____ JEP#:_____
WHY WE CRIED:_____
_____

BOOK TITLE:_____ JEP#:_____

WHY WE CRIED:_____

_____

BOOK TITLE:_____ JEP#:_____

WHY WE CRIED:_____

_____

BOOK TITLE:_____ JEP#:_____

WHY WE CRIED:_____

_____

BOOK TITLE:_____ JEP#:_____

WHY WE CRIED:_____

_____

BOOK TITLE:_____ JEP#:_____

WHY WE CRIED:_____

_____

BOOK TITLE:_____ JEP#:_____

WHY WE CRIED:_____

_____

BOOK TITLE:_____ JEP#:_____

WHY WE CRIED:_____

_____

BOOK TITLE:_____ JEP#:_____

WHY WE CRIED:_____

_____

BOOK TITLE:_____ JEP#:_____

WHY WE CRIED:_____

_____

BOOK TITLE:_____ JEP#:_____

WHY WE CRIED:_____

_____

BOOK TITLE:_____ JEP#:_____

WHY WE CRIED:_____

BOOK TITLE:_____ JEP#:_____
WHY WE CRIED:_____

BOOK TITLE:_____ JEP#:_____
WHY WE CRIED:_____

BOOK TITLE:_____ JEP#:_____
WHY WE CRIED:_____

BOOK TITLE:_____ JEP#:_____
WHY WE CRIED:_____

BOOK TITLE:_____ JEP#:_____
WHY WE CRIED:_____

BOOK TITLE:_____ JEP#:_____
WHY WE CRIED:_____

BOOK TITLE:_____ JEP#:_____
WHY WE CRIED:_____

BOOK TITLE:_____ JEP#:_____
WHY WE CRIED:_____

BOOK TITLE:_____ JEP#:_____
WHY WE CRIED:_____

BOOK TITLE:_____ JEP#:_____
WHY WE CRIED:_____

BOOK TITLE:_____ JEP#:_____

BOOKS THAT CHANGED US

*"Books are the bees which carry the quickening pollen
from one to another mind."*
— JAMES RUSSELL LOWELL

Stories can change our lives. They can change how we see ourselves, how we see other people, how we see the world we live in. They can inspire us to change for the better in some way. They can give us examples to live by. Stories can be like little birds that build their nests in our souls and remain there, singing their songs for the rest of our lives. They can shape us. They can make us more compassionate. More understanding. More heroic. More loyal. More merciful. More selfless. More loving. As you journey through the world of books, you will sometimes encounter stories that change you. Remember those stories. Embrace them. Let them do their work. Return to them many times throughout your life. Here is a place where you can remember those stories that somehow reached into your heart and made you a little different than you were before.

BOOK TITLE:_____ JEP#:_____
HOW THIS STORY CHANGED US:_____
_____

BOOK TITLE:_____ JEP#:_____
HOW THIS STORY CHANGED US:_____
_____

BOOK TITLE:_____ JEP#:_____
HOW THIS STORY CHANGED US:_____
_____

BOOK TITLE:_____ JEP#:_____
HOW THIS STORY CHANGED US:_____
_____

BOOK TITLE:_____ JEP#:_____
HOW THIS STORY CHANGED US:_____
_____

BOOK TITLE:_____ JEP#:_____
HOW THIS STORY CHANGED US:_____
_____

BOOK TITLE:_____ JEP#:_____
HOW THIS STORY CHANGED US:_____
_____

BOOK TITLE:_____ JEP#:_____

HOW THIS STORY CHANGED US:_____

_____

BOOK TITLE:_____ JEP#:_____

HOW THIS STORY CHANGED US:_____

_____

BOOK TITLE:_____ JEP#:_____

HOW THIS STORY CHANGED US:_____

_____

BOOK TITLE:_____ JEP#:_____

HOW THIS STORY CHANGED US:_____

_____

BOOK TITLE:_____ JEP#:_____

HOW THIS STORY CHANGED US:_____

_____

BOOK TITLE:_____ JEP#:_____

HOW THIS STORY CHANGED US:_____

_____

BOOK TITLE:_____ JEP#:_____

HOW THIS STORY CHANGED US:_____

_____

BOOK TITLE:_____ JEP#:_____

HOW THIS STORY CHANGED US:_____

_____

BOOK TITLE:_____ JEP#:_____

HOW THIS STORY CHANGED US:_____

_____

BOOK TITLE:_____ JEP#:_____

HOW THIS STORY CHANGED US:_____

_____

BOOK TITLE:_____ JEP#:_____

HOW THIS STORY CHANGED US:_____

_____

BOOK TITLE:_____ JEP#:_____

HOW THIS STORY CHANGED US:_____

_____

BOOK TITLE:_____ JEP#:_____

HOW THIS STORY CHANGED US:_____

_____

BOOK TITLE:_____ JEP#:_____

HOW THIS STORY CHANGED US:_____

_____

BOOK TITLE:_____ JEP#:_____

HOW THIS STORY CHANGED US:_____

_____

BOOK TITLE:_____ JEP#:_____

HOW THIS STORY CHANGED US:_____

_____

BOOK TITLE:_____ JEP#:_____

HOW THIS STORY CHANGED US:_____

_____

BOOK TITLE:_____ JEP#:_____

HOW THIS STORY CHANGED US:_____

_____

BOOK TITLE:_____ JEP#:_____

HOW THIS STORY CHANGED US:_____

_____

BOOK TITLE:_____ JEP#:_____

HOW THIS STORY CHANGED US:_____

_____

BOOK TITLE:_____ JEP#:_____

HOW THIS STORY CHANGED US:_____
_____

BOOK TITLE:_____ JEP#:_____

HOW THIS STORY CHANGED US:_____
_____

BOOK TITLE:_____ JEP#:_____

HOW THIS STORY CHANGED US:_____
_____

BOOK TITLE:_____ JEP#:_____

HOW THIS STORY CHANGED US:_____
_____

BOOK TITLE:_____ JEP#:_____

HOW THIS STORY CHANGED US:_____
_____

BOOK TITLE:_____ JEP#:_____

HOW THIS STORY CHANGED US:_____
_____

BOOK TITLE:_____ JEP#:_____

HOW THIS STORY CHANGED US:_____
_____

BOOK TITLE:_____ JEP#:_____

HOW THIS STORY CHANGED US:_____
_____

BOOK TITLE:_____ JEP#:_____

HOW THIS STORY CHANGED US:_____
_____

BOOK TITLE:_____ JEP#:_____

HOW THIS STORY CHANGED US:_____
_____

OUR VERY FAVORITE BOOKS!

"If a book is well written, I always find it too short."
— JANE AUSTEN, *Sense and Sensibility*

This is a list not just of good books, but of those few wonderful stories that are so special they become your family's very, very favorites. Some of these titles might be on your other lists as well. That's wonderful! What an honor for a writer to have their book remembered on more than one of your lists. Remember though, that not every book can make it onto this elite list; only the ones that are your absolute favorites. So talk through it with your family before you write a book title here!

BOOK TITLE:_____ JEP#:_____
WHY WE LOVE IT!:_____
_____

BOOK TITLE:_____ JEP#:_____
WHY WE LOVE IT!:_____
_____

BOOK TITLE:_____ JEP#:_____
WHY WE LOVE IT!:_____
_____

BOOK TITLE:_____ JEP#:_____
WHY WE LOVE IT!:_____
_____

BOOK TITLE:_____ JEP#:_____
WHY WE LOVE IT!:_____
_____

BOOK TITLE:_____ JEP#:_____
WHY WE LOVE IT!:_____
_____

BOOK TITLE:_____ JEP#:_____
WHY WE LOVE IT!:_____
_____

BOOK TITLE:_____ JEP#:_____
WHY WE LOVE IT!:_____
_____

BOOK TITLE:_____ JEP#:_____

WHY WE LOVE IT!:_____

_____

BOOK TITLE:_____ JEP#:_____

WHY WE LOVE IT!:_____

_____

BOOK TITLE:_____ JEP#:_____

WHY WE LOVE IT!:_____

_____

BOOK TITLE:_____ JEP#:_____

WHY WE LOVE IT!:_____

_____

BOOK TITLE:_____ JEP#:_____

WHY WE LOVE IT!:_____

_____

BOOK TITLE:_____ JEP#:_____

WHY WE LOVE IT!:_____

_____

BOOK TITLE:_____ JEP#:_____

WHY WE LOVE IT!:_____

_____

BOOK TITLE:_____ JEP#:_____

WHY WE LOVE IT!:_____

_____

BOOK TITLE:_____ JEP#:_____

WHY WE LOVE IT!:_____

_____

BOOK TITLE:_____ JEP#:_____

WHY WE LOVE IT!:_____

_____

BOOK TITLE:_____ JEP#:_____

WHY WE LOVE IT!:_____

_____

BOOK TITLE:_____ JEP#:_____

WHY WE LOVE IT!:_____

_____

BOOK TITLE:_____ JEP#:_____

WHY WE LOVE IT!:_____

_____

BOOK TITLE:_____ JEP#:_____

WHY WE LOVE IT!:_____

_____

BOOK TITLE:_____ JEP#:_____

WHY WE LOVE IT!:_____

_____

BOOK TITLE:_____ JEP#:_____

WHY WE LOVE IT!:_____

_____

BOOK TITLE:_____ JEP#:_____

WHY WE LOVE IT!:_____

_____

BOOK TITLE:_____ JEP#:_____

WHY WE LOVE IT!:_____

_____

BOOK TITLE:_____ JEP#:_____

WHY WE LOVE IT!:_____

_____

BOOK TITLE:_____ JEP#:_____

WHY WE LOVE IT!:_____

_____

BOOK TITLE:_____ JEP#:_____

WHY WE LOVE IT!:_____

_____

BOOK TITLE:_____ JEP#:_____

WHY WE LOVE IT!:_____

_____

BOOK TITLE:_____ JEP#:_____

WHY WE LOVE IT!:_____

_____

BOOK TITLE:_____ JEP#:_____

WHY WE LOVE IT!:_____

_____

BOOK TITLE:_____ JEP#:_____

WHY WE LOVE IT!:_____

_____

BOOK TITLE:_____ JEP#:_____

WHY WE LOVE IT!:_____

_____

BOOK TITLE:_____ JEP#:_____

WHY WE LOVE IT!:_____

_____

BOOK TITLE:_____ JEP#:_____

WHY WE LOVE IT!:_____

_____

BOOK TITLE:_____ JEP#:_____

WHY WE LOVE IT!:_____

_____

BOOK TITLE:_____ JEP#:_____

WHY WE LOVE IT!:_____

_____

ADVENTURE QUESTS

ADVENTURE QUESTS are special book adventures for you to pursue with your family. Each Quest has a theme, so look through all of them and pick one that really interests you! Your Quest will have a list of goals that must be completed. When you finish a goal, check the box beside it. When you've checked all the boxes, you've completed that Quest. Color in the special Quest Shield to show your accomplishment.

Some ADVENTURE QUESTS will be easier than others, but all of them will send you off to discover wonderful new books and stories you've never read before. If you enjoy a particular Quest and want to explore it further, move on to the BONUS QUEST. Some Quests also have SUB-QUESTS and a few even have ARCH-ADVENTURER QUESTS (for the most brave and adventurous readers!).

NOTE: Several of the ARCH-ADVENTURER QUESTS require more record-keeping than your *Stories We Shared* book journal has space for. You'll need to keep track of these on separate sheets of paper. We recommend that you tape or glue a folder or large envelope inside the back cover of this journal to store your additional lists in.

2ND NOTE: When you're filling out an ADVENTURE QUEST form and you see a space to write the JEP#, that's short for "Journal Entry Page #." That just means the page number in the main journal section of *Stories We Shared* where you recorded that book's information. When you go on an ADVENTURE QUEST, you won't record as much information as you do in the main journal section. Writing down the book's JEP# on the ADVENTURE QUEST form will give you a quick way to cross-reference the title.

QUEST LIST

World Explorers . . . . PG 162
Time Travelers . . . . PG 164
Genre Hoppers . . . . PG 166
The Serial Bookworm . . . . . . PG 168
The Literary Zookeeper . . . . . PG 169
High Adventure . . . . PG 171
Myths & Legends . . . . PG 173
Brainstormers . . . . PG 175
Newbery Quest . . . . PG 176
Caldecott Quest . . . . PG 181

> "In my contact with people, I find that, as a rule, it is only the little, narrow people who live for themselves, who never read good books, who do not travel, who never open up their souls in a way to permit them to come into contact with other souls – with the great outside world."
> — BOOKER T. WASHINGTON, *Up From Slavery*

WORLD EXPLORERS
See the world without leaving your house!

☐ **QUEST:** Read books or stories by authors from **20** different countries.

COUNTRY:_____ BOOK TITLE:_____ JEP#:_____

COUNTRY:_____ BOOK TITLE:_____ JEP#:_____

COUNTRY:_____ BOOK TITLE:_____ JEP#:_____

COUNTRY:_____ BOOK TITLE:_____ JEP#:_____

COUNTRY:_____ BOOK TITLE:_____ JEP#:_____

COUNTRY:_____ BOOK TITLE:_____ JEP#:_____

COUNTRY:_____ BOOK TITLE:_____ JEP#:_____

COUNTRY:_____ BOOK TITLE:_____ JEP#:_____

COUNTRY:_____ BOOK TITLE:_____ JEP#:_____

COUNTRY:_____ BOOK TITLE:_____ JEP#:_____

COUNTRY:_____ BOOK TITLE:_____ JEP#:_____

COUNTRY:_____ BOOK TITLE:_____ JEP#:_____

COUNTRY:_____ BOOK TITLE:_____ JEP#:_____

COUNTRY:_____ BOOK TITLE:_____ JEP#:_____

COUNTRY:_____ BOOK TITLE:_____ JEP#:_____

COUNTRY:_____ BOOK TITLE:_____ JEP#:_____

COUNTRY:_____ BOOK TITLE:_____ JEP#:_____

COUNTRY:_____ BOOK TITLE:_____ JEP#:_____

COUNTRY:_____ BOOK TITLE:_____ JEP#:_____

COUNTRY:_____ BOOK TITLE:_____ JEP#:_____

WORLD EXPLORERS SUB-QUEST:

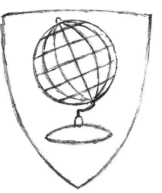

☐ Read books by authors from 6 different continents:
North America, South America, Africa, Europe, Asia, Australia.

CONTINENT: _____ BOOK TITLE: _____ JEP#:_____

CONTINENT: _____ BOOK TITLE: _____ JEP#:_____

CONTINENT: _____ BOOK TITLE: _____ JEP#:_____

CONTINENT: _____ BOOK TITLE: _____ JEP#:_____

CONTINENT: _____ BOOK TITLE: _____ JEP#:_____

CONTINENT: _____ BOOK TITLE: _____ JEP#:_____

WORLD EXPLORERS BONUS QUEST:

☐ Read a book or story that was written in Antarctica!

BOOK TITLE:_____ JEP #: _____

WORLD EXPLORERS ARCH-ADVENTURER QUEST:

☐ If you liked the World Explorers challenge, why not keep going as far as you can with it? There are fewer than 200 countries in the world today. Would it even be possible to read a book or story from each one of them? Do you dare to even try?

[There's not enough space here, so you'll need to keep track of these on a different sheet of paper.]

"The reading of all good books is like conversation with
the finest men of past centuries."
— RENÉ DESCARTES

TIME TRAVELERS
Buckle into your time machine and get ready to go!

QUEST: COMPLETE EACH OF THE FOLLOWING MISSIONS.

☐ Read a book written the year you were born. (Pick a different book for each child. Use extra paper as necessary).

BOOK TITLE:_____ YEAR WRITTEN:_____ JEP#: _____

BOOK TITLE:_____ YEAR WRITTEN:_____ JEP#: _____

BOOK TITLE:_____ YEAR WRITTEN:_____ JEP#: _____

BOOK TITLE:_____ YEAR WRITTEN:_____ JEP#: _____

☐ Read a book that one of your grandparents (or an older relative or family friend) loved when they were a child.

BOOK RECOMMENDED BY:_____

BOOK TITLE:_____ YEAR WRITTEN:_____ JEP#: _____

☐ Read a book written approximately 100 years ago.

BOOK TITLE:_____ YEAR WRITTEN:_____ JEP#: _____

☐ Read a book written more than 1000 years ago.

BOOK TITLE:_____ YEAR WRITTEN:_____ JEP#: _____

☐ Read a book or story that was written (or told) sometime before the year 1 A.D.

BOOK TITLE:_____ YEAR WRITTEN:_____ JEP#: _____

☐ Read a story that was set in the future when it was written, but is now in the past.

BOOK TITLE:_____ YEAR WRITTEN:_____ JEP#: _____

YEAR (OR TIME PERIOD) STORY WAS SET IN:_____

☐ Read a story that is set at least 100 years from now in the future.

BOOK TITLE:_____ YEAR WRITTEN:_____ JEP#: _____

YEAR (OR TIME PERIOD) STORY WAS SET IN:_____

TIME TRAVELERS SUB-QUEST:

☐ Read 6 books or stories set during the times of different **GREAT EVENTS** in the world. "Great" doesn't always mean "good." It means important, or far-reaching in its effects. These could be events like World War I, or the Moon Landing, or The Great Fire of London, or the Black Plague, or the Enlightenment, or the end of the reign of the Last Emperor of China, or the life of an influential religious or political leader, or the completion of the Transcontinental Railway. All of these are just examples to get you thinking. You can discuss with your family what you believe are some of the great events in history, and decide which ones you want to read about together in stories that are set in those times and places.

GREAT EVENT:_____

BOOK TITLE:_____ JEP#: _____

GREAT EVENT:_____

BOOK TITLE:_____ JEP#: _____

GREAT EVENT:_____

BOOK TITLE:_____ JEP#: _____

GREAT EVENT:_____

BOOK TITLE:_____ JEP#: _____

GREAT EVENT:_____

BOOK TITLE:_____ JEP#: _____

GREAT EVENT:_____

BOOK TITLE:_____ JEP#: _____

TIME TRAVELERS ARCH-ADVENTURER QUEST:

☐ Read books or stories that were either written in or are set in each century from the 1st through the 21st.

NOTE: There's not enough space here, so you'll need to keep track of these on a new sheet of paper. You also might want to make a timeline to show when these stories were written and when they were set.

"All that mankind has done, thought, gained, or been;
it is lying as in magic preservation in the pages of books."
— THOMAS CARLYLE, *On Heroes: Six Lectures*

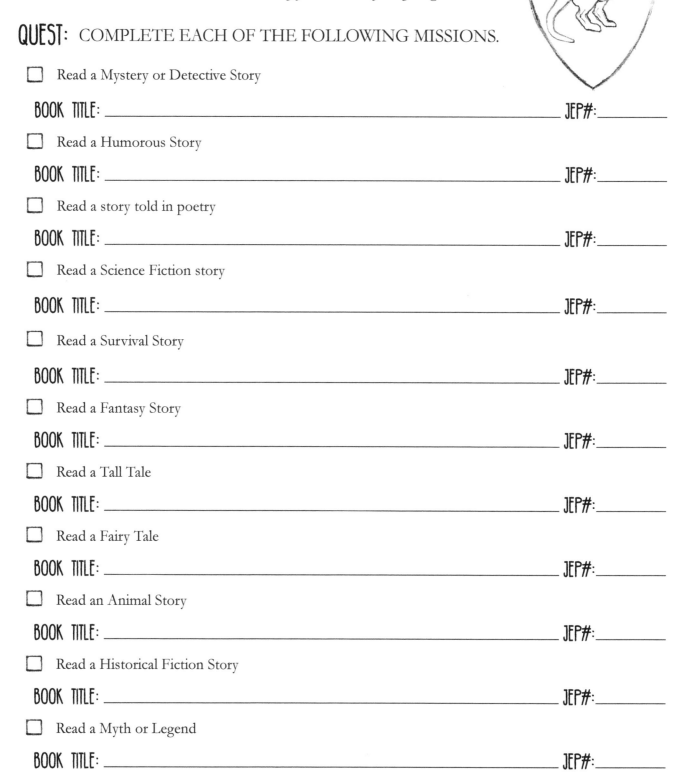

GENRE HOPPERS
Get ready for a little bit of everything!

QUEST: COMPLETE EACH OF THE FOLLOWING MISSIONS.

☐ Read a Mystery or Detective Story

BOOK TITLE: _____ JEP#:_____

☐ Read a Humorous Story

BOOK TITLE: _____ JEP#:_____

☐ Read a story told in poetry

BOOK TITLE: _____ JEP#:_____

☐ Read a Science Fiction story

BOOK TITLE: _____ JEP#:_____

☐ Read a Survival Story

BOOK TITLE: _____ JEP#:_____

☐ Read a Fantasy Story

BOOK TITLE: _____ JEP#:_____

☐ Read a Tall Tale

BOOK TITLE: _____ JEP#:_____

☐ Read a Fairy Tale

BOOK TITLE: _____ JEP#:_____

☐ Read an Animal Story

BOOK TITLE: _____ JEP#:_____

☐ Read a Historical Fiction Story

BOOK TITLE: _____ JEP#:_____

☐ Read a Myth or Legend

BOOK TITLE: _____ JEP#:_____

GENRE HOPPERS SUB-QUEST: Stories Told in Other Forms

☐ Read a story written as a Play
(If you already know how to read, ask to be assigned a part!)

PLAY TITLE:_____ PLAYWRIGHT:_____

☐ Listen to a recording of a skilled storyteller telling (not reading!) a story.

STORY TITLE: _____ STORYTELLER:_____

☐ Read a story portrayed in Graphic Novel or Comic Book form.

BOOK TITLE: _____ JEP#:_____

☐ Read a book or story that was made into a movie. Watch the movie together afterwards.

BOOK TITLE: _____ JEP#:_____

GENRE HOPPERS BONUS QUEST:

☐ Read a book or story that is a satire, parody, or spoof of a whole genre
(or even of a specific book or story). Fairy Tales are a great place to start,
because there are lots of Fairy Tale parodies! NOTE: Parodies are usually
funnier if you've read the serious version of the story first.

BOOK TITLE: _____ JEP#:_____

AUTHOR: _____ PARODY OF: _____

GENRE HOPPERS ARCH-ADVENTURER QUEST:

☐ Not all books fall into a single genre. Some are combinations of genres.
For instance, a story about a dog that gets lost when its owners are moving,
and that then travels a thousand miles to find them again, would be an Animal Story
and a Survival Story. Or there might be Science Fiction story about a Detective solving
a crime on another planet. Or a Historical Fiction story told through Poetry. You get the idea. Your
ARCH-ADVENTURER QUEST is to find and read **10** books or stories that fit into more than one
genre. Sometimes people call these kinds of stories *Mashups*. NOTE: There are more genres than the
ones listed in the GENRE HOPPER QUEST. (Westerns, for instance.) A parent or librarian can help
you discover even more rewarding genres to explore.

[There's not enough space here, so you'll need to keep track of these on a new sheet of paper.]

"The person who deserves most pity is a lonesome one on a rainy day who doesn't know how to read."
— BENJAMIN FRANKLIN

THE SERIAL BOOKWORM
How long does it take to chew through a whole shelf of books?

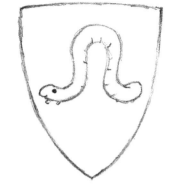

QUEST: COMPLETE EACH OF THE FOLLOWING MISSIONS.

☐ Read a book and then read its sequel. An example of this would be *Alice's Adventures in Wonderland* followed by the sequel *Through the Looking Glass*. (In some cases, the follow-up book is actually a **prequel**, but that's okay too!)

BOOK TITLE: _____ JEP#:_____

SEQUEL (or PREQUEL) TITLE: _____ JEP#:_____

☐ Read a trilogy.

BOOK 1 TITLE: _____ JEP#:_____

BOOK 2 TITLE: _____ JEP#:_____

BOOK 3 TITLE: _____ JEP#:_____

☐ Read a complete series of 5 books (or more!).

SERIES NAME:_____

AUTHOR:_____ JEP#s:_____

THE SERIAL BOOKWORM SUB-QUEST:

☐ Can you find and read a series (of any length) that was started by one author, but completed by another? Can you tell a difference in the writing style of the earlier book(s) vs. the later one(s)?

SERIES NAME: _____ JEP#s:_____

AUTHOR #1: _____ AUTHOR #2: _____

THE SERIAL BOOKWORM ARCH-ADVENTURER QUEST:

☐ Read a book series that includes 10 books or more!

SERIES NAME: _____ AUTHOR:_____

JEP#s:_____

"Do you know, I always thought unicorns were fabulous monsters, too? I never saw one alive before!"
"Well, now that we have seen each other," said the unicorn, "if you'll believe in me, I'll believe in you."
— LEWIS CARROLL, *Through the Looking Glass*

THE LITERARY ZOOKEEPER
A private menagerie on your bookshelf!

QUEST: COMPLETE EACH OF THE FOLLOWING MISSIONS.

☐ Read **10** stories that each features a different species of animal.

ANIMAL:_____ BOOK TITLE:_____ JEP#:_____

ANIMAL:_____ BOOK TITLE:_____ JEP#:_____

ANIMAL:_____ BOOK TITLE:_____ JEP#:_____

ANIMAL:_____ BOOK TITLE:_____ JEP#:_____

ANIMAL:_____ BOOK TITLE:_____ JEP#:_____

ANIMAL:_____ BOOK TITLE:_____ JEP#:_____

ANIMAL:_____ BOOK TITLE:_____ JEP#:_____

ANIMAL:_____ BOOK TITLE:_____ JEP#:_____

ANIMAL:_____ BOOK TITLE:_____ JEP#:_____

ANIMAL:_____ BOOK TITLE:_____ JEP#:_____

☐ Read a book or story set in a zoo.

BOOK TITLE: _____ JEP#:_____

☐ Read **3** books or stories in which animals are the first-person narrators.

BOOK TITLE: _____ JEP#:_____

KIND OF ANIMAL: _____ AUTHOR:_____

BOOK TITLE: _____ JEP#:_____

KIND OF ANIMAL: _____ AUTHOR:_____

BOOK TITLE: _____ JEP#:_____

KIND OF ANIMAL: _____ AUTHOR:_____

The LITERARY ZOOKEEPER **SUB-QUEST**:

☐ Read at least **5** books about imaginary kinds of animals.
(i.e. Unicorn, Dragon, Pegasus, Faun, Phoenix, etc.)

IMAGINARY ANIMAL: _____ JEP#:_____

BOOK TITLE: _____ AUTHOR:_____

IMAGINARY ANIMAL: _____ JEP#:_____

BOOK TITLE: _____ AUTHOR:_____

IMAGINARY ANIMAL: _____ JEP#:_____

BOOK TITLE: _____ AUTHOR:_____

IMAGINARY ANIMAL: _____ JEP#:_____

BOOK TITLE: _____ AUTHOR:_____

IMAGINARY ANIMAL: _____ JEP#:_____

BOOK TITLE: _____ AUTHOR:_____

The LITERARY ZOOKEEPER **ARCH-ADVENTURER QUEST**:

☐ Write an adventure story about your own pet, or about an animal you've
encountered somewhere. Read the story aloud to your family. If you're not
old enough to write yet, tell your story to someone who can write it down
for you, and then ask them to read it aloud to the rest of your family.

[There's not enough space here, so you'll need to write your story on a different sheet of paper.]

"To live will be an awfully big adventure."
— J. M. BARRIE, *Peter Pan*

HIGH ADVENTURE
Rip-roaring yarns and derring-do!

QUEST: COMPLETE THE FOLLOWING MISSIONS.

☐ Read a book or story about Pirates.

BOOK TITLE: _____ JEP#:_____

☐ Read a book or story about Knights.

BOOK TITLE: _____ JEP#:_____

☐ Read a book or story about Pioneers.

BOOK TITLE: _____ JEP#:_____

☐ Read a book or story about Explorers.

BOOK TITLE: _____ JEP#:_____

☐ Read a book or story about Detectives.

BOOK TITLE: _____ JEP#:_____

☐ Read a book or story about Spies.

BOOK TITLE: _____ JEP#:_____

☐ Read a book or story about Soldiers.

BOOK TITLE: _____ JEP#:_____

☐ Read a book or story about a Hero (from Myth, Legend, or Real Life).

BOOK TITLE: _____ JEP#:_____

☐ Read a book or story about Vikings.

BOOK TITLE: _____ JEP#:_____

☐ Read a book or story about Treasure Hunters.

BOOK TITLE: _____ JEP#:_____

HIGH ADVENTURE SUB-QUEST:

☐ Make a list of four additional categories of people (besides those already listed in the main quest) that would be exciting to read about. Read a book or story about each of them.

PEOPLE CATEGORY: _____

BOOK TITLE: _____ JEP#:_____

PEOPLE CATEGORY: _____

BOOK TITLE: _____ JEP#:_____

PEOPLE CATEGORY: _____

BOOK TITLE: _____ JEP#:_____

PEOPLE CATEGORY: _____

BOOK TITLE: _____ JEP#:_____

HIGH ADVENTURE ARCH-ADVENTURER QUEST:

☐ Read an entire book series about Pioneers, Knights, Treasure Hunters, or one of the other "High Adventure" Quest categories!

SERIES ABOUT:_____

SERIES TITLE: _____ JEP#s:_____

HIGH ADVENTURE ACTIVITY QUEST:

☐ Hide a "treasure" and then make a treasure map or a list of clues for other people to follow!

"The more truly we can see life as a fairytale, the more clearly the tale resolves
itself into war with the dragon who is wasting fairyland."
— G. K. CHESTERTON, *The New Jerusalem*

MYTHS AND LEGENDS
*What's not to love about outrageous story twists and
larger-than-life heroes and villains?*

QUEST: COMPLETE THE FOLLOWING MISSIONS.

☐ Read a Greek Myth or Legend

BOOK TITLE: _____ JEP#:_____

☐ Read a Roman Myth or Legend

BOOK TITLE: _____ JEP#:_____

☐ Read a Celtic Myth or Legend

BOOK TITLE: _____ JEP#:_____

☐ Read a Native American Myth or Legend

BOOK TITLE: _____ JEP#:_____

☐ Read a Norse Myth or Legend

BOOK TITLE: _____ JEP#:_____

☐ Read a Jewish Myth or Legend

BOOK TITLE: _____ JEP#:_____

☐ Read an Arabian Myth or Legend

BOOK TITLE: _____ JEP#:_____

☐ Read a Russian Myth or Legend

BOOK TITLE: _____ JEP#:_____

☐ Read a German Myth or Legend

BOOK TITLE: _____ JEP#:_____

MYTHS AND LEGENDS Quest Continues On Next Page!

☐ Read a Central or South American Myth or Legend

BOOK TITLE: _____ JEP#:_____

☐ Read a Mexican Myth or Legend

BOOK TITLE: _____ JEP#:_____

☐ Read a Chinese Myth or Legend

BOOK TITLE: _____ JEP#:_____

☐ Read a Japanese Myth or Legend

BOOK TITLE: _____ JEP#:_____

☐ Read an African Myth or Legend

BOOK TITLE: _____ JEP#:_____

☐ Read an Australian Myth or Legend

BOOK TITLE: _____ JEP#:_____

☐ Read an Egyptian Myth or Legend

BOOK TITLE: _____ JEP#:_____

MYTHS & LEGENDS SUB-QUEST:

☐ Read a book that is a collection of Myths & Legends
from a single culture or people group.

CULTURE OR PEOPLE GROUP:_____

BOOK TITLE: _____ JEP#:_____

FAVORITE STORY IN THE COLLECTION: _____

MYTHS & LEGENDS ARCH-ADVENTURER QUEST:

☐ Read Myths or Legends from 10 additional cultures or people groups.

[There's not enough space here, so you'll need to keep track of these on a different sheet of paper.]

"I've got the key to my castle in the air,
but whether I can unlock the door remains to be seen."
—LOUISA MAY ALCOTT, *Little Women*

BRAINSTORMERS:
CREATE YOUR OWN QUEST!
Put on your thinking cap and let those creative juices flow!

Brainstorm ideas together to create your own original Reading Quest, Sub-Quest, and Arch-Adventurer Quest. Write down each of the goals on this page (beside the check boxes) and design your own shield. Then venture forth, brave readers, and fulfill your Quest! (Use extra sheets of paper if you need to.)

_____ QUEST:

☐ _____

_____

_____

_____

_____

_____

_____ SUB-QUEST:

☐ _____

_____

_____

_____ ARCH-ADVENTURER QUEST:

☐ _____

_____

_____

> "Literature is a luxury; fiction is a necessity."
> — G. K. CHESTERTON, *The Defendant*

NEWBERY QUEST
Some of the most celebrated books through the years!

The Newbery Medal has been awarded every year since 1922 to recognize "the most distinguished American children's book published the previous year," as chosen by the Newbery Medal Committee. It is a great honor for an author to have their book nominated, and an even greater honor to win.

☐ **QUEST:** Read **20** Newbery Medal Winning Books

MEDAL YEAR:_____ BOOK TITLE:_____ JEP#:_____

MEDAL YEAR:_____ BOOK TITLE:_____ JEP#:_____

MEDAL YEAR:_____ BOOK TITLE:_____ JEP#:_____

MEDAL YEAR:_____ BOOK TITLE:_____ JEP#:_____

MEDAL YEAR:_____ BOOK TITLE:_____ JEP#:_____

MEDAL YEAR:_____ BOOK TITLE:_____ JEP#:_____

MEDAL YEAR:_____ BOOK TITLE:_____ JEP#:_____

MEDAL YEAR:_____ BOOK TITLE:_____ JEP#:_____

MEDAL YEAR:_____ BOOK TITLE:_____ JEP#:_____

MEDAL YEAR:_____ BOOK TITLE:_____ JEP#:_____

MEDAL YEAR:_____ BOOK TITLE:_____ JEP#:_____

MEDAL YEAR:_____ BOOK TITLE:_____ JEP#:_____

MEDAL YEAR:_____ BOOK TITLE:_____ JEP#:_____

MEDAL YEAR:_____ BOOK TITLE:_____ JEP#:_____

MEDAL YEAR:_____ BOOK TITLE:_____ JEP#:_____

MEDAL YEAR:_____ BOOK TITLE:_____ JEP#:_____

MEDAL YEAR:_____ BOOK TITLE:_____ JEP#:_____

MEDAL YEAR:_____ BOOK TITLE:_____ JEP#:_____

MEDAL YEAR:_____ BOOK TITLE:_____ JEP#:_____

MEDAL YEAR:_____ BOOK TITLE:_____ JEP#:_____

NEWBERY SUB-QUEST:

☐ Pick a year. Read the Newbery Medal Winner for that year. Then read the Newbery Honor Books for that year as well. (Newbery Honor Books are those that were also nominated for the medal, but didn't receive the top award.) Discuss whether you think the Newbery judges made the best choice that year.

MEDAL YEAR:_____

NEWBERY WINNER: _____ JEP#:_____

NEWBERY HONOR BOOK: _____ JEP#:_____

NEWBERY HONOR BOOK: _____ JEP#:_____

NEWBERY HONOR BOOK: _____ JEP#:_____

NEWBERY HONOR BOOK: _____ JEP#:_____

NEWBERY HONOR BOOK: _____ JEP#:_____

NEWBERY ARCH-ADVENTURER QUEST:

☐ Read EVERY Newbery Award-Winning Book!

NEWBERY MEDAL WINNERS

☐ 1922: THE STORY OF MANKIND by Hendrik Willem van Loon (LIVERIGHT)
☐ 1923: THE VOYAGES OF DOCTOR DOLITTLE by Hugh Lofting (STOKES)
☐ 1924: THE DARK FRIGATE by Charles Hawes (LITTLE, BROWN)
☐ 1925: TALES FROM SILVER LANDS by Charles Finger (DOUBLEDAY)
☐ 1926: SHEN OF THE SEA by Arthur Bowie Chrisman (DUTTON)
☐ 1927: SMOKY, THE COWHORSE by Will James (SCRIBNER)
☐ 1928: GAY NECK, THE STORY OF A PIGEON by Dhan Gopal Mukerji (DUTTON)
☐ 1929: THE TRUMPETER OF KRAKOW by Eric P. Kelly (MACMILLAN)
☐ 1930: HITTY, HER FIRST HUNDRED YEARS by Rachel Field (MACMILLAN)
☐ 1931: THE CAT WHO WENT TO HEAVEN by Elizabeth Coatsworth (MACMILLAN)
☐ 1932: WATERLESS MOUNTAIN by Laura Adams Armer (LONGMANS)
☐ 1933: YOUNG FU OF THE UPPER YANGTZE by Elizabeth Lewis (WINSTON)
☐ 1934: INVINCIBLE LOUISA: THE STORY OF THE AUTHOR OF LITTLE WOMEN by Cornelia Meigs (LITTLE, BROWN)
☐ 1935: DOBRY by Monica Shannon (VIKING)
☐ 1936: CADDIE WOODLAWN by Carol Ryrie Brink (MACMILLAN)
☐ 1937: ROLLER SKATES by Ruth Sawyer (VIKING)
☐ 1938: THE WHITE STAG by Kate Seredy (VIKING)
☐ 1939: THIMBLE SUMMER by Elizabeth Enright (RINEHART)
☐ 1940: DANIEL BOONE by James Daugherty (VIKING)

(NEWBERY QUEST Continued on Next Page!)

- [ ] 1941: CALL IT COURAGE by Armstrong Sperry (MACMILLAN)
- [ ] 1942: THE MATCHLOCK GUN by Walter Edmonds (DODD)
- [ ] 1943: ADAM OF THE ROAD by Elizabeth Janet Gray (VIKING)
- [ ] 1944: JOHNNY TREMAIN by Esther Forbes (HOUGHTON)
- [ ] 1945: RABBIT HILL by Robert Lawson (VIKING)
- [ ] 1946: STRAWBERRY GIRL by Lois Lenski (LIPPINCOTT)
- [ ] 1947: MISS HICKORY by Carolyn Sherwin Bailey (VIKING)
- [ ] 1948: THE TWENTY-ONE BALLOONS by William Péne du Bois (VIKING)
- [ ] 1949: KING OF THE WIND by Marguerite Henry (RAND MCNALLY)
- [ ] 1950: THE DOOR IN THE WALL by Marguerite de Angeli (DOUBLEDAY)
- [ ] 1951: AMOS FORTUNE, FREE MAN by Elizabeth Yates (DUTTON)
- [ ] 1952: GINGER PYE by Eleanor Estes (HARCOURT)
- [ ] 1953: SECRET OF THE ANDES by Ann Nolan Clark (VIKING)
- [ ] 1954: ...AND NOW MIGUEL by Joseph Krumgold (CROWELL)
- [ ] 1955: THE WHEEL ON THE SCHOOL by Meindert DeJong (HARPER)
- [ ] 1956: CARRY ON, MR. BOWDITCH by Jean Lee Latham (HOUGHTON)
- [ ] 1957: MIRACLES ON MAPLE HILL by Virginia Sorensen (HARCOURT)
- [ ] 1958: RIFLES FOR WATIE by Harold Keith (CROWELL)
- [ ] 1959: THE WITCH OF BLACKBIRD POND by Elizabeth George Speare (HOUGHTON)
- [ ] 1960: ONION JOHN by Joseph Krumgold (CROWELL)
- [ ] 1961: ISLAND OF THE BLUE DOLPHINS by Scott O'Dell (HOUGHTON)
- [ ] 1962: THE BRONZE BOW by Elizabeth George Speare (HOUGHTON)
- [ ] 1963: A WRINKLE IN TIME by Madeleine L'Engle (FARRAR)
- [ ] 1964: IT'S LIKE THIS, CAT by Emily Neville (HARPER)
- [ ] 1965: SHADOW OF A BULL by Maia Wojciechowska (ATHENEUM)
- [ ] 1966: I, JUAN DE PAREJA by Elizabeth Borton de Trevino (FARRAR)
- [ ] 1967: UP A ROAD SLOWLY by Irene Hunt (FOLLETT)
- [ ] 1968: FROM THE MIXED-UP FILES OF MRS. BASIL E. FRANKWEILER by E.L. Konigsburg (ATHENEUM)
- [ ] 1969: THE HIGH KING by Lloyd Alexander (HOLT)
- [ ] 1970: SOUNDER by William H. Armstrong (HARPER)
- [ ] 1971: SUMMER OF THE SWANS by Betsy Byars (VIKING)
- [ ] 1972: MRS. FRISBY AND THE RATS OF NIMH by Robert C. O'Brien (ATHENEUM)
- [ ] 1973: JULIE OF THE WOLVES by Jean Craighead George (HARPER)
- [ ] 1974: THE SLAVE DANCER by Paula Fox (BRADBURY)
- [ ] 1975: M. C. HIGGINS, THE GREAT by Virginia Hamilton (MACMILLAN)
- [ ] 1976: THE GREAY KING by Susan Cooper (MCELDERRY/ATHENEUM)
- [ ] 1977: ROLL OF THUNDER, HEAR MY CRY by Mildred D. Taylor (DIAL)
- [ ] 1978: BRIDGE TO TERABITHIA by Katherine Paterson (CROWELL)
- [ ] 1979: THE WESTING GAME by Ellen Raskin (DUTTON)
- [ ] 1980: A GATHERING OF DAYS: A NEW ENGLAND GIRL'S JOURNAL, 1830-1832 by Joan W. Blos (SCRIBNER)
- [ ] 1981: JACOB HAVE I LOVED by Katherine Paterson (CROWELL)
- [ ] 1982: A VISIT TO WILLIAM BLAKE'S INN: POEMS FOR INNOCENT AND EXPERIENCED TRAVELERS by Nancy Willard (HARCOURT)
- [ ] 1983: DICEY'S SONG by Cynthia Voigt (ATHENEUM)
- [ ] 1984: DEAR MR. HENSHAW by Beverly Cleary (MORROW)
- [ ] 1985: THE HERO AND THE CROWN by Robin McKinley (GREENWILLOW)
- [ ] 1986: SARAH, PLAIN AND TALL by Patricia MacLachlan (HARPER)

- [ ] 1987: THE WHIPPING BOY by Sid Fleischman (GREENWILLOW)
- [ ] 1988: LINCOLN: A PHOTOBIOGRAPHY by Russell Freedman (CLARION)
- [ ] 1989: JOYFUL NOISE: POEMS FOR TWO VOICES by Paul Fleischman (HARPER)
- [ ] 1990: NUMBER THE STARS by Lois Lowry (HOUGHTON)
- [ ] 1991: MANIAC MAGEE by Jerry Spinelli (LITTLE, BROWN)
- [ ] 1992: SHILOH by Phyllis Reynolds Naylor (ATHENEUM)
- [ ] 1993: MISSING MAY by Cynthia Rylant (JACKSON/ORCHARD)
- [ ] 1994: THE GIVER by Lois Lowry (HOUGHTON)
- [ ] 1995: WALK TWO MOONS by Sharon Creech (HARPERCOLLINS)
- [ ] 1996: THE MIDWIFE'S APPRENTICE by Karen Cushman (CLARION)
- [ ] 1997: THE VIEW FROM SATURDAY by E.L. Konigsburg (JEAN KARL/ATHENEUM)
- [ ] 1998: OUT OF THE DUST by Karen Hesse (SCHOLASTIC)
- [ ] 1999: HOLES by Louis Sachar (FRANCES FOSTER)
- [ ] 2000: BUD, NOT BUDDY by Christopher Paul Curtis (DELACORTE)
- [ ] 2001: A YEAR DOWN YONDER by Richard Peck (DIAL)
- [ ] 2002: A SINGLE SHARD by Linda Sue Park (CLARION BOOKS/HOUGHTON MIFFLIN)
- [ ] 2003: CRISPIN: THE CROSS OF LEAD by Avi (HYPERION BOOKS FOR CHILDREN)
- [ ] 2004: THE TALE OF DESPEREAUX: BEING THE STORY OF A MOUSE, A PRINCESS, SOME SOUP, AND A SPOOL OF THREAD by Kate DiCamillo (CANDLEWICK PRESS)
- [ ] 2005: KIRA-KIRA by Cynthia Kadohata (ATHENEUM BOOKS FOR YOUNG READERS/SIMON & SCHUSTER)
- [ ] 2006: CRISS CROSS by Lynne Rae Perkins (GREENWILLOW BOOKS/HARPERCOLLINS)
- [ ] 2007: THE HIGHER POWER OF LUCKY by Susan Patron; illus. by Matt Phelan (SIMON & SCHUSTER/RICHARD JACKSON)
- [ ] 2008: GOOD MASTERS! SWEET LADIES! VOICES FROM A MEDIEVAL VILLAGE by Laura Amy Schlitz (CANDLEWICK)
- [ ] 2009: THE GRAVEYARD BOOK by Neil Gaiman; illus. by David McKean (HARPERCOLLINS)
- [ ] 2010: WHEN YOU REACH ME by Rebecca Stead (WENDY LAMB BOOKS, AN IMPRINT OF RANDOM HOUSE CHILDREN'S BOOKS)
- [ ] 2011: MOON OVER MANIFEST by Clare Vanderpool (DELACORTE PRESS, AN IMPRINT OF RANDOM HOUSE CHILDREN'S BOOKS)
- [ ] 2012: DEAD END IN NORVELT by Jack Gantos (FARRAR STRAUS GIROUX)
- [ ] 2013: THE ONE AND ONLY IVAN by Katherine Applegate (HARPERCOLLINS CHILDREN'S BOOKS)
- [ ] 2014: FLORA & ULYSSES: THE ILLUMINATED ADVENTURES by Kate DeCamillo (CANDLEWICK PRESS)
- [ ] 2015: THE CROSSOVER by Kwame Alexander (HOUGHTON MIFFLIN HARCOURT)
- [ ] 2016: LAST STOP ON MARKET STREET by Matt de la Peña (G.P. PUTNAM'S SONS/PENGUIN)
- [ ] 2017: THE GIRL WHO DRANK THE MOON by Kelly Barnhill (ALGONQUIN YOUNG READERS, AN IMPRINT OF ALGONQUIN BOOKS)
- [ ] 2018: _____
- [ ] 2019: _____
- [ ] 2020: _____
- [ ] 2021: _____
- [ ] 2022: _____
- [ ] 2023: _____
- [ ] 2024: _____
- [ ] 2025: _____
- [ ] 2026: _____
- [ ] 2027: _____

☐ 2028: _____

☐ 2029: _____

☐ 2030: _____

☐ 2031: _____

☐ 2032: _____

☐ 2033: _____

☐ 2034: _____

☐ 2035: _____

☐ 2036: _____

☐ 2037: _____

☐ 2038: _____

☐ 2039: _____

☐ 2040: _____

☐ 2041: _____

☐ 2042: _____

☐ 2043: _____

☐ 2044: _____

☐ 2045: _____

☐ 2046: _____

☐ 2047: _____

☐ 2048: _____

☐ 2049: _____

☐ 2050: _____

☐ 2051: _____

☐ 2052: _____

☐ 2053: _____

☐ 2054: _____

☐ 2055: _____

☐ 2056: _____

☐ 2057: _____

☐ 2058: _____

☐ 2059: _____

CALDECOTT QUEST

If you love illustrated stories, this quest is for you!

The Caldecott Medal has been awarded every year since 1938 to the "artist of the most distinguished American Picture Book for Children published in the United States during the preceding year." The winner is chosen by members of the Newbery Medal Committee. It is, of course, a great honor for an illustrator to have their book nominated, and an even greater honor to win.

☐ **QUEST:** Read **20** Caldecott Medal Winning Books

MEDAL YEAR:_____ BOOK TITLE:_____ JEP#:_____

MEDAL YEAR:_____ BOOK TITLE:_____ JEP#:_____

MEDAL YEAR:_____ BOOK TITLE:_____ JEP#:_____

MEDAL YEAR:_____ BOOK TITLE:_____ JEP#:_____

MEDAL YEAR:_____ BOOK TITLE:_____ JEP#:_____

MEDAL YEAR:_____ BOOK TITLE:_____ JEP#:_____

MEDAL YEAR:_____ BOOK TITLE:_____ JEP#:_____

MEDAL YEAR:_____ BOOK TITLE:_____ JEP#:_____

MEDAL YEAR:_____ BOOK TITLE:_____ JEP#:_____

MEDAL YEAR:_____ BOOK TITLE:_____ JEP#:_____

MEDAL YEAR:_____ BOOK TITLE:_____ JEP#:_____

MEDAL YEAR:_____ BOOK TITLE:_____ JEP#:_____

MEDAL YEAR:_____ BOOK TITLE:_____ JEP#:_____

MEDAL YEAR:_____ BOOK TITLE:_____ JEP#:_____

MEDAL YEAR:_____ BOOK TITLE:_____ JEP#:_____

MEDAL YEAR:_____ BOOK TITLE:_____ JEP#:_____

MEDAL YEAR:_____ BOOK TITLE:_____ JEP#:_____

MEDAL YEAR:_____ BOOK TITLE:_____ JEP#:_____

MEDAL YEAR:_____ BOOK TITLE:_____ JEP#:_____

MEDAL YEAR:_____ BOOK TITLE:_____ JEP#:_____

CALDECOTT SUB-QUEST:

☐ Pick a year and read not just the Caldecott Award Winner for that year, but the Caldecott Honor Books for that year as well. (Caldecott Honor Books are those that were also nominated for the medal, but didn't receive the top award.) Discuss whether you think the Caldecott judges made the best choice that year.

MEDAL YEAR: _____

CALDECOTT WINNER: _____ JEP#:_____

CALDECOTT HONOR BOOK: _____ JEP#:_____

CALDECOTT HONOR BOOK: _____ JEP#:_____

CALDECOTT HONOR BOOK: _____ JEP#:_____

CALDECOTT HONOR BOOK: _____ JEP#:_____

CALDECOTT HONOR BOOK: _____ JEP#:_____

CALDECOTT ARCH-ADVENTURER QUEST:

☐ Read EVERY Caldecott Award-Winning Book!

CALDECOTT MEDAL WINNERS

☐ 1938: ANIMALS OF THE BIBLE, A PICTURE BOOK illus. by Dorothy P. Lathrop; text: selected by Helen Dean Fish (LIPPINCOTT)

☐ 1939: MEI LI by Thomas Handforth (DOUBLEDAY)

☐ 1940: ABRAHAM LINCOLN by Ingri & Edgar Parin d'Aulaire (DOUBLEDAY)

☐ 1941: THEY WERE STRONG AND GOOD by Robert Lawson (VIKING)

☐ 1942: MAKE WAY FOR DUCKLINGS by Robert McCloskey (VIKING)

☐ 1943: THE LITTLE HOUSE by Virginia Lee Burton (HOUGHTON)

☐ 1944: MANY MOONS illus. by Louis Slobodkin; text: James Thurber (HARCOURT)

☐ 1945: PRAYER FOR A CHILD illus. by Elizabeth Orton Jones; text: Rachel Field (MACMILLAN)

☐ 1946: THE ROOSTER CROWS by Maud & Miska Petersham (MACMILLAN)

☐ 1947: THE LITTLE ISLAND illus. by Leonard Weisgard; text: Golden MacDonald, pseud. [Margaret Wise Brown] (DOUBLEDAY)

☐ 1948: WHITE SNOW, BRIGHT SNOW illus. by Roger Duvoisin; text: Alvin Tresselt (LOTHROP)

☐ 1949: THE BIG SNOW by Berta & Elmer Hader (MACMILLAN)

☐ 1950: SONG OF THE SWALLOWS by Leo Politi (SCRIBNER)

☐ 1951: THE EGG TREE by Katherine Milhous (SCRIBNER)

☐ 1952: FINDERS KEEPERS illus. by Nicolas (Nicholas Mordvinoff); text by Will (William Lipkind) (HARCOURT)

☐ 1953: THE BIGGEST BEAR by Lynd Ward (HOUGHTON)

☐ 1954: MADELINE'S RESCUE by Ludwig Bemelmans (VIKING)

- [ ] 1955: CINDERELLA, OR THE LITTLE GLASS SLIPPER illus. by Marcia Brown;
text: translated from Charles Perrault by Marcia Brown (SCRIBNER)
- [ ] 1956: FROG WENT A-COURTIN' illus. by Feodor Rojankovsky; text: retold by John Langstaff (HARCOURT)
- [ ] 1957: A TREE IS NICE illus. by Marc Simont; text: Janice Udry (HARPER)
- [ ] 1958: TIME OF WONDER by Robert McCloskey (VIKING)
- [ ] 1959: CHANTICLEER AND THE FOX illus. by Barbara Cooney;
text: adapted from Chaucer's Canterbury Tales by Barbara Cooney (CROWELL)
- [ ] 1960: NINE DAYS TO CHRISTMAS illus. by Marie Hall Ets; text: Marie Hall Ets & Aurora Labastida (VIKING)
- [ ] 1961: BABOUSHKA AND THE THREE KINGS illus. by Nicolas Sidjakov; text: Ruth Robbins (PARNASSUS)
- [ ] 1962: ONCE A MOUSE retold and illus. by Marcia Brown (SCRIBNER)
- [ ] 1963: THE SNOWY DAY by Ezra Jack Keats (VIKING)
- [ ] 1964: WHERE THE WILD THINGS ARE by Maurice Sendak (HARPER)
- [ ] 1965: MAY I BRING A FRIEND? illus. by Beni Montresor; text: Beatrice Schenk de Regniers (ATHENEUM)
- [ ] 1966: ALWAYS ROOM FOR ONE MORE illus. by Nonny Hogrogian;
text: Sorche Nic Leodhas, pseud. [Leclair Alger] (HOLT)
- [ ] 1967: SAM, BANGS & MOONSHINE by Evaline Ness (HOLT)
- [ ] 1968: DRUMMER HOFF illus. by Ed Emberley; text: adapted by Barbara Emberley (PRENTICE-HALL)
- [ ] 1969: THE FOOL OF THE WORLD AND THE FLYING SHIP illus. by Uri Shulevitz;
text: retold by Arthur Ransome (FARRAR)
- [ ] 1970: SYLVESTER AND THE MAGIC PEBBLE by William Steig (WINDMILL BOOKS)
- [ ] 1971: A STORY A STORY retold and illus. by Gail E. Haley (ATHENEUM)
- [ ] 1972: ONE FINE DAY retold and illus. by Nonny Hogrogian (MACMILLAN)
- [ ] 1973: THE FUNNY LITTLE WOMAN illus. by Blair Lent; text; retold by Arlene Mosel (DUTTON)
- [ ] 1974: DUFFY AND THE DEVIL illus. by Margot Zemach; retold by Harve Zemach (FARRAR)
- [ ] 1975: ARROW TO THE SUN by Gerald McDermott (VIKING)
- [ ] 1976: WHY MOSQUITOES BUZZ IN PEOPLE'S EARS illus. by Leo & Diane Dillon;
text: retold by Verna Aardema (DIAL)
- [ ] 1977: ASHANTI TO ZULU: AFRICAN TRADITIONS illus. by Leo & Diane Dillon; text: Margaret Musgrove (DIAL)
- [ ] 1978: NOAH'S ARK by Peter Spier (DOUBLEDAY)
- [ ] 1979: THE GIRL WHO LOVED WILD HORSES by Paul Goble (BRADBURY)
- [ ] 1980: OX-CART MAN illus. by Barbara Cooney; text: Donald Hall (VIKING)
- [ ] 1981: FABLES by Arnold Lobel (HARPER)
- [ ] 1982: JUMANJI by Chris Van Allsburg (HOUGHTON)
- [ ] 1983: SHADOW translated and illus. by Marcia Brown; original text in French; Blaise Cendrars (SCRIBNER)
- [ ] 1984: THE GLORIOUS FLIGHT: ACROSS THE CHANNEL WITH LOUIS BLERIOT by Alice & Martin Provensen (VIKING)
- [ ] 1985: SAINT GEORGE AND THE DRAGON illus. by Trina Schart Hyman; text: retold by Margaret Hodges (LITTLE, BROWN)
- [ ] 1986: THE POLAR EXPRESS by Chris Van Allsburg (HOUGHTON)
- [ ] 1987: HEY, AL illus by Richard Egielski; text: Arthur Yorinks (FARRAR)
- [ ] 1988: OWL MOON illus. by John Schoenherr; text: Jane Yolen (PHILOMEL)
- [ ] 1989: SONG AND DANCE MAN illus. by Stephen Gammell; text: Karen Ackerman (KNOPF)
- [ ] 1990: LON PO PO: A RED-RIDING HOOD STORY FROM CHINA by Ed Young (PHILOMEL)
- [ ] 1991: BLACK AND WHITE by David Macaulay (HOUGHTON)
- [ ] 1992: TUESDAY by David Wiesner (CLARION BOOKS)
- [ ] 1993: MIRETTE ON THE HIGH WIRE by Emily Arnold McCully (PUTNAM)
- [ ] 1994: GRANDFATHER'S JOURNEY illus. by Allen Say; text: edited by Walter Lorraine (HOUGHTON)
- [ ] 1995: SMOKY NIGHT illus. by David Diaz; text: Eve Bunting (HARCOURT)
- [ ] 1996: OFFICER BUCKLE AND GLORIA by Peggy Rathmann (PUTNAM)

(CALDECOTT QUEST Continued on Next Page!)

☐ 1997: GOLEM by David Wisniewski (CLARION)

☐ 1998: RAPUNZEL by Paul O. Zelinsky (DUTTON)

☐ 1999: SNOWFLAKE BENTLEY illus. by Mary Azarian, written by Jacqueline Briggs Martin (HOUGHTON)

☐ 2000: JOSEPH HAD A LITTLE OVERCOAT by Simms Taback (VIKING)

☐ 2001: SO YOU WANT TO BE PRESIDENT? illus. by David Small, Written by Judith St. George (PHILOMEL BOOKS)

☐ 2002: THE THREE PIGS by David Wiesner (CLARION/HOUGHTON MIFFLIN)

☐ 2003: MY FRIEND RABBIT by Eric Rohmann (ROARING BROOK PRESS/MILLBROOK PRESS)

☐ 2004: THE MAN WHO WALKED BETWEEN THE TOWERS by Mordicai Gerstein (ROARING BROOK PRESS/MILLBROOK PRESS)

☐ 2005: KITTEN'S FIRST FULL MOON by Kevin Henkes (GREENWILLOW BOOKS/HARPERCOLLINS PUBLISHERS)

☐ 2006: THE HELLO, GOODBYE WINDOW illus. by Chris Raschka, written by Norton Juster (MICHAEL DI CAPUA/HYPERION)

☐ 2007: FLOTSAM by David Wiesner (CLARION)

☐ 2008: THE INVENTION OF HUGO CABRET by Brian Selznick (SCHOLASTIC PRESS, AN IMPRINT OF SCHOLASTIC)

☐ 2009: THE HOUSE IN THE NIGHT illus. by Beth Krommes, written by Susan Marie Swanson (HOUGHTON MIFFLIN COMPANY)

☐ 2010: THE LION & THE MOUSE by Jerry Pinkney (LITTLE, BROWN AND COMPANY)

☐ 2011: A SICK DAY FOR AMOS MCGEE illus. by Erin E. Stead, written by Phillip C. Stead
   (NEAL PORTER BOOKS/ROARING BROOK PRESS, AN IMPRINT OF MACMILLAN CHILDREN'S PUBLISHING GROUP)

☐ 2012: A BALL FOR DAISY by Chris Raschka (SCHWARTZ & WADE BOOKS, AN IMPRINT OF RANDOM HOUSE CHILDREN'S BOOKS,
   A DIVISION OF RANDOM HOUSE, INC.)

☐ 2013: THIS IS NOT MY HAT by Jon Klassen (CANDLEWICK PRESS)

☐ 2014: LOCOMOTIVE by Brian Floca (ATHENIUM BOOKS FOR YOUNG READERS, AN IMPRINT OF SIMON & SCHUSTER CHILDREN'S PUBLISHING)

☐ 2015: THE ADVENTURES OF BEEKLE: THE UNIMAGINARY FRIEND by Dan Santat
   (LITTLE, BROWN AND COMPANY, A DIVISION OF HACHETTE BOOK GROUP, INC.)

☐ 2016: FINDING WINNIE: THE TRUE STORY OF THE WORLD'S MOST FAMOUS BEAR illus. by Sophie Blackall,
   written by Lindsay Mattick (LITTLE, BROWN AND COMPANY, A DIVISION OF HACHETTE BOOK GROUP, INC.)

☐ 2017: RADIANT CHILD: THE STORY OF YOUNG ARTIST JEAN-MICHEL BASQUIAT illus. & written by Javaka Steptoe
   (LITTLE, BROWN AND COMPANY, A DIVISION OF HACHETTE BOOK GROUP, INC.)

☐ 2018: _____

☐ 2019: _____

☐ 2020: _____

☐ 2021: _____

☐ 2022: _____

☐ 2023: _____

☐ 2024: _____

☐ 2025: _____

☐ 2026: _____

☐ 2027: _____

☐ 2028: _____

☐ 2029: _____

☐ 2030: _____

☐ 2031: _____

☐ 2032: _____

- ☐ 2033: _____
- ☐ 2034: _____
- ☐ 2035: _____
- ☐ 2036: _____
- ☐ 2037: _____
- ☐ 2038: _____
- ☐ 2039: _____
- ☐ 2040: _____
- ☐ 2041: _____
- ☐ 2042: _____
- ☐ 2043: _____
- ☐ 2044: _____
- ☐ 2045: _____
- ☐ 2046: _____
- ☐ 2047: _____
- ☐ 2048: _____
- ☐ 2049: _____
- ☐ 2050: _____
- ☐ 2051: _____
- ☐ 2052: _____
- ☐ 2053: _____
- ☐ 2054: _____
- ☐ 2055: _____
- ☐ 2056: _____
- ☐ 2057: _____
- ☐ 2058: _____
- ☐ 2059: _____

AUTHORS WE MET!

If you collect the autographs of well-known people your hobby is called *philography*. Signatures of famous or influential people can become very valuable over time. A photo signed by Albert Einstein, for instance, once sold for $75,000, and a baseball signed by Babe Ruth sold for $388,375!

Of course most signatures, even of well-known people, will never be worth that much money, but they're still fun to collect and a wonderful way to remember interesting people you meet.

This section gives you a place to collect author autographs and to keep track of when and where you met them. Some signatures are difficult to read, so be sure to clearly print the author's name in the "Author Name" space!

Authors aren't so difficult to find. Many writers travel around to give talks at bookstores, schools, libraries, conferences, and book fairs. Most of them enjoy meeting people who have read and appreciated their books. And most of them will be delighted to give you their autograph if you ask. So don't be shy! When you meet an author, tell them something you like about their stories, and ask them to sign their name here in your book journal. Who knows, maybe you'll even become friends.

SIGNATURE:_____ DATE:_____

AUTHOR NAME:_____ LOCATION: _____

FAVORITE BOOK BY THIS AUTHOR: _____ JEP#:_____

SIGNATURE:_____ DATE:_____

AUTHOR NAME:_____ LOCATION: _____

FAVORITE BOOK BY THIS AUTHOR: _____ JEP#:_____

SIGNATURE:_____ DATE:_____

AUTHOR NAME:_____ LOCATION: _____

FAVORITE BOOK BY THIS AUTHOR: _____ JEP#:_____

SIGNATURE:_____ DATE:_____

AUTHOR NAME:_____ LOCATION: _____

FAVORITE BOOK BY THIS AUTHOR: _____ JEP#:_____

SIGNATURE:_____ DATE:_____

AUTHOR NAME:_____ LOCATION: _____

FAVORITE BOOK BY THIS AUTHOR: _____ JEP#:_____

SIGNATURE:_____ DATE:_____

AUTHOR NAME:_____ LOCATION: _____

FAVORITE BOOK BY THIS AUTHOR: _____ JEP#:_____

SIGNATURE:_____ DATE:_____

AUTHOR NAME:_____ LOCATION: _____

FAVORITE BOOK BY THIS AUTHOR: _____ JEP#:_____

SIGNATURE:_____ DATE:_____

AUTHOR NAME:_____ LOCATION: _____

FAVORITE BOOK BY THIS AUTHOR: _____ JEP#:_____

SIGNATURE:_____ DATE:_____

AUTHOR NAME:_____ LOCATION: _____

FAVORITE BOOK BY THIS AUTHOR: _____ JEP#:_____

SIGNATURE:_____ DATE:_____

AUTHOR NAME:_____ LOCATION: _____

FAVORITE BOOK BY THIS AUTHOR: _____ JEP#:_____

SIGNATURE:_____ DATE:_____

AUTHOR NAME:_____ LOCATION: _____

FAVORITE BOOK BY THIS AUTHOR: _____ JEP#:_____

SIGNATURE:_____ DATE:_____

AUTHOR NAME:_____ LOCATION: _____

FAVORITE BOOK BY THIS AUTHOR: _____ JEP#:_____

SIGNATURE:_____ DATE:_____

AUTHOR NAME:_____ LOCATION: _____

FAVORITE BOOK BY THIS AUTHOR: _____ JEP#:_____

SIGNATURE:_____ DATE:_____

AUTHOR NAME:_____ LOCATION: _____

FAVORITE BOOK BY THIS AUTHOR: _____ JEP#:_____

SIGNATURE:_____ DATE:_____

AUTHOR NAME:_____ LOCATION: _____

FAVORITE BOOK BY THIS AUTHOR: _____ JEP#:_____

SIGNATURE:_____ DATE:_____

AUTHOR NAME:_____ LOCATION: _____

FAVORITE BOOK BY THIS AUTHOR: _____ JEP#:_____

SIGNATURE:_____ DATE:_____

AUTHOR NAME:_____ LOCATION: _____

FAVORITE BOOK BY THIS AUTHOR: _____ JEP#:_____

SIGNATURE:_____ DATE:_____

AUTHOR NAME:_____ LOCATION: _____

FAVORITE BOOK BY THIS AUTHOR: _____ JEP#:_____

SIGNATURE:_____ DATE:_____

AUTHOR NAME:_____ LOCATION: _____

FAVORITE BOOK BY THIS AUTHOR: _____ JEP#:_____

SIGNATURE:_____ DATE:_____

AUTHOR NAME:_____ LOCATION: _____

FAVORITE BOOK BY THIS AUTHOR: _____ JEP#:_____

SIGNATURE:_____ DATE:_____

AUTHOR NAME:_____ LOCATION: _____

FAVORITE BOOK BY THIS AUTHOR: _____ JEP#:_____

SIGNATURE:_____ DATE:_____

AUTHOR NAME:_____ LOCATION: _____

FAVORITE BOOK BY THIS AUTHOR: _____ JEP#:_____

ABOUT THE CREATORS OF THIS JOURNAL

THE AUTHOR

Douglas Kaine McKelvey has meandered merrily through the last two decades as a father, author, essayist, scriptwriter, poet, and song lyricist. His published works include *The Places Beyond the Maps* (a novel-length story included in Andrew Peterson's compilation *The Wingfeather Tales*), a middle-grade reader titled *The Angel Knew Papa and the Dog*, 3 picture books, a collection of poetry, and more than 300 recorded songs. Douglas dwells in the long shadows south of Nashville, Tennessee with his Norwegianish wife and their 3 semi-Norwegianish daughters. His digital essence has been captured at www.dougmckelvey.com.

THE ILLUSTRATOR

Jamin (JAY-min) Still spent his childhood writing and drawing and dreaming, and when he woke one perfect spring morning to discover that he had become an adult, he saw no good reason to change his happy ways. He studied painting, literature, and writing in college and now spends his days painting and dreaming and writing. His first published picture book was *Ellen and the Winter Wolves*. Jamin roosts in a little stone house with his wife and young son in the magical town of Wichita, Kansas (which is rumored to be near one of the few remaining portals to Oz). You can visit him online at www.jaminstill.com.

THE COLLABORATION

Douglas and Jamin met suspiciously at a shadowy sort of conference and instantly became fans of one another's work. They first collaborated on *The Wishes of the Fish King*, a picture book published in late 2016 by Rabbit Room Press. Pairing lyrical text with magical paintings, *The Wishes of the Fish King* recounts the story of a little girl and her father and mother as they journey by foot and boat through the story-book wonders of the world they share—a world where field and forest and fairy tale blend. *The Wishes of the Fish King* is a quiet celebration of wonder and love for generations to read aloud, share, and delight in together. *Stories We Shared: A Family Book Journal* is an idea Douglas and Jamin began to develop together while working on their picture book.

Printed in the USA
CPSIA information can be obtained
at www.ICGtesting.com
JSHW070457081123
51566JS00003B/15